Mountain of Fire and Miracles Ministries
International Headquarters,
Lagos, Nigeria.

DELIVERANCE THROUGH THE WATCHES FOR SEXUAL PERVERSION

A PROGRAMME
THAT RUNS THROUGHOUT A WHOLE DAY
AT 3 HOUR INTERVALS

The Prayer Watches are as follows:
1st - 6am | 2nd - 9am | 3rd - 12 noon
4th - 3pm | 5th - 6pm | 6th - 9pm | 7th - 12am

This gives a total of
7 Prayer Watches.

DELIVERANCE THROUGH
THE WATCHES FOR SEXUAL
PERVERSION
© 2011 DR. D. K.OLUKOYA
ISBN **9780615990071**
Reprinted: January 2013

Published by:

Mountain of Fire and Miracles Ministries Press
13, Olasimbo Street, Onike, Yaba, Lagos.
I salute *my wonderful* wife Pastor Shade *for her* invaluable support in the ministry. I appreciate her unquantifiable support in the book ministry as the cover designer, art editor and art advisor,

All Scripture quotation is from the King James

Bible
S T U D Y
1

HEARING FROM GOD

BIBLE STUDY 1

HEARING FROM GOD

A. HOW GOD COMMUNICATES

God communicates with us and reveals Himself to us:

THROUGH REVELATION: (Psalm 19:1; Isa. 40:26; Rom. 1:19-20; 2:15. Revelation the uncovering or unveiling of information.

THROUGH INSPIRATION: That is, when the Holy Spirit acts on man to make known God's revelation (Job 32:8).

THROUGH ILLUMINATION: This is a ministry of the Holy Spirit which enables those of us who are in right standing with God to understand revelations, as they pertain to our individual lives.

B. HOW DO WE KNOW THE VOICE OF GOD?

To know the voice of God, we must

1. Commit our lives completely to the Lord.

2. Learn to test our impressions.
3. Be honest with ourselves and have faith.
4. Let God have access to every area of our lives.
5. Pray to God to open our faculties to receive His messages.

C. WHEN GOD SPEAKS TO YOU,

1. It will glorify His name.
2. It will cause you to worship Him.
3. It will agree with the Scriptures.
4. It will impart His knowledge to you.
5. It will cause you to love others and Him more.
6. It can produce a response to God in prayer, praise, thanksgiving, worship or confessions.

D. VEHICLES OF DIVINE COMMUNICATIONS:

1. Face to face in a two-way communication (Gen. 3:9; Exod. 33:11).
2. By a voice (Num. 11:17; Exod. 3:2-4; 1 Sam. 3:4).
3. By dreams (Gen. 20:6; Matt. 1:20; Acts 2:17).
4. By open visions (Acts 10:1-6; 12:7-11).
5. By closed visions (Acts 16:9:18:9-10).
6. By trance (Acts 10:9-16).
7. By angels (Luke 1:11-20, 27-28; Acts 8:26-29; Gen. 16:7; 19:1).

REVELATION IS AN UNVEILING OF INFORMATION

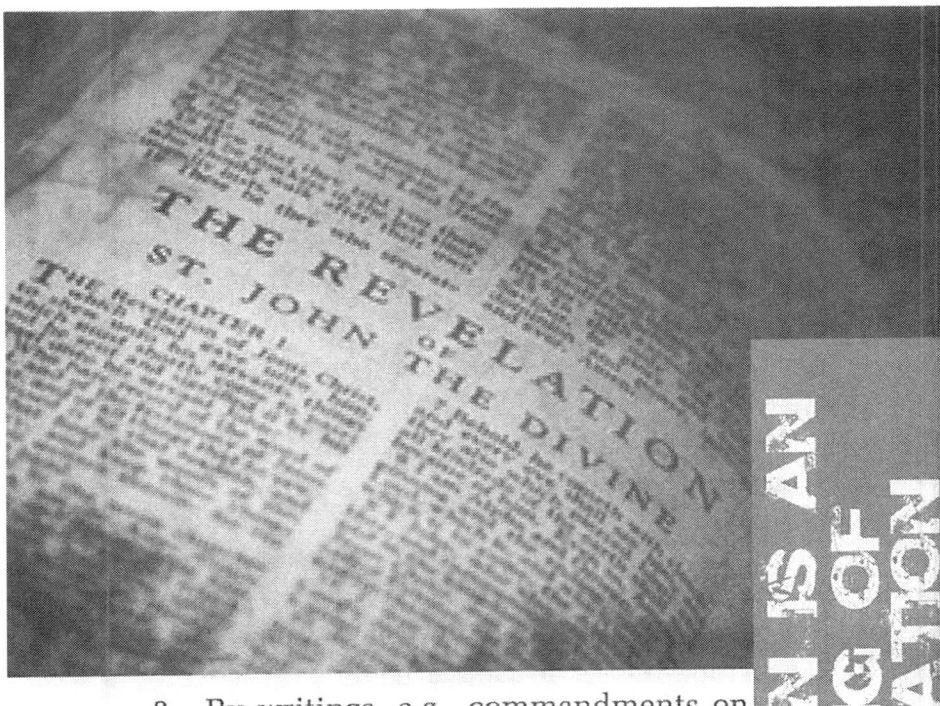

8. By writings, e.g., commandments on stone tablets, sentences written on the wall (Exod. 20; Dan. 5:5).

9. By miracles (Exod. 14:21; 7: 7-11; 2 Kings 5:1-17)

10. Through the written Word (The Gospels).

11. Reference to Bible passages.

12. Anointed messages and teachings.

13. Anointed counsellings.

14. Walking with holy men and women (Prov. 13:20).

15. Anointed music (2 Kings 3:15).

16. Anointed meditations.

17. Conscience.
18. Burdens of the heart.
19. Divine ideas.
20. Intuition (knowing signals).
21. Internal understanding.
22. Impression on the heart.
23. Inward witness.
24. Inner voice.
25. Outer voice (Acts 9:4-9).
26. Closed outer voice (1 Sam. 3:3-10).
27. Still small voice (1 Kings 19:12).
28. Sudden impulse.
29. Favourable and positive circumstances (Gen. 24:15-48).
30. Difficult circumstances (Deut. 8).
31. Words of wisdom.
32. Words of knowledge.
33. Faith.
34. Healing.
35. Working of miracles.
36. Prophecy.
37. Discerning of spirits.
38. Diverse kinds of tongues.

39. Interpretation of tongues.
40. Remembering the truth.
41. Intercession from within.
42. Conclusive evidence (by their fruits).
43. Divine visitation.
44. Symbolic actions (Jer. 18).

E. POWER PRINCIPLES OF HEARING FROM GOD:

1. Salvation (John 10:3-4).
2. Brokenness (John 12:24).
3. Receptivity (Rev. 3:20; John 8:43; Matt. 17:5).
4. Faith (John 10:3,27; Heb. 11:6; 4:2; Rom. 10:17).
5. Attentiveness (1 Sam. 3:1-11; Exod. 3:4).
6. Discernment (John 12:26-29; 1 Kings 19:11-13).
7. Obedience.

F. WHY GOD SPEAKS

1. To warn you of an impending danger - Acts 27:10.
2. To give you the picture of your destiny - Gen. 37:5-10.
3. To reveal the secrets of your enemy - 2 Kings 6:15-17.
4. To correct you - Job 5:17.
5. To carry out an assignment for Him - Jonah 1:1-2.
6. To intercede for others - Ezek. 22:30.

When God speaks to you...
...It will agree with Scriptures.

7. To work for Him - Acts 26:16-18.
8. To give you a piece of information - 1 Sam. 3:4-13.
9. To show that He loves you - Gen. 18:17-23.
10. To ask you a question - Gen. 3:9.
11. To mete out a punishment - Dan. 4:3-32.
12. To prosper you - Deut. 28:1-3.
13. To deliver you from your problems - Acts 12:7.
14. To teach you certain lessons - Exod. 24:12.
15. To create things - Gen. 1:3-31.
16. To reveal the past to you - Moses (The book of Genesis).
17. To reveal the present to you - (Gen. 19:27-28).
18. To reveal the future to you - John (Rev. 1:1-20).
19. To approve certain things - Luke 9:35.
20. To bless you - Gen. 32:26-30.
21. To caution you - 2 Sam. 12:7-11.
22. To provide for your needs - 1 Kg. 17:2-4.

23. To heal you - John 5:5-9.
24. To have a covenant with you - Gen. 15:18.
25. To anoint you - Luke 4:18.
26. To take you from darkness to light - Acts 9:4-6.

ADVANTAGES OF HEARING FROM GOD:

1. Joy in your heart.
2. Proof that you are a privileged/ peculiar person.
3. Satan fears you.
4. Your life becomes organised.
5. Your prosperity is guaranteed.
6. You will not move with unprofitable people.
7. Makes you have a peace of mind.
8. Respect from people.
9. You will receive the blue-print of your life.
10. You will know the secrets of God and man.
11. You will become spiritually sound.

HOW GOD SPEAKS

1. Face to face in a two-way communication - Here, God talks with you directly and you reply Him immediately in an open conversation. He talked to Adam and Eve and they replied (Gen. 3:8-19). He with Abraham and he replied (Gen. 18:17,23-33). Moses and God had a discussion (Exod. 3:4-22; 31:18).

2. *The written Word/Bible* - 2 Tim. 3:16: "All scripture is given by inspiration of God, and is profitable for doctrine, for reproof, for correction, for instruction in righteousness:" The Bible is the Word and voice of God. As we read it, the Lord is talking with us.

3. *Reference to passages* - When someone or the Holy Spirit refers you to Bible passages. Jesus referred satan to certain Bible passages (Luke 4:4,8,12).

4. *Anointed messages/teachings* - The sermons of an anointed minister and the teachings of an anointed teacher convey the mind of God (1Cor. 1:17-18; Acts 26:28).

5. *Anointed counsellings* - As an anointed counsellor counsels you, you are listening to God (as Jethro counsels Moses - Exod. 18:14-23).

6. *Jumpy Bible verses* - When a particular Scripture magnetises your spirit and you begin to meditate on it, God is talking with you directly (Acts 8:26-39)

7. *Walking with holy men or women* - The lifestyle of a holy man speaks the voice of God. The life of Abraham prospered Lot; the life of Moses prospered Joshua; the life of Paul prospered Timothy.

THOSE WHO RECOGNISED THE VOICE OF GOD:

1. The ground (Numbers 16:27-32).
2. Animals - e.g. the snake (Gen. 3:14), the bear - (2Kings 2:24).
3. Trees (Mark 11:20-22).
4. The dead (John 11:43-44.)
5. Demons (Matt. 8:28-32).
6. Light (Gen. 1:3).
7. Water (2 Kings 2:21-22).
8. Winds (Matt. 8:23-27).
9. Mountains (Matt. 21:21).
10. Diseases and sicknesses (Mark 1:40-42).
11. Infirmity (Luke 13:11-13).
12. Rivers, hills, valleys and forests (Ezek. 6:1-3).
13. Food - Mark 6:38-43.
14. Cooking pot and bottle of oil (1 Kings 17:14-16).

THE WORD OF GOD CAME TO THE FOLLOWING:

1. Abraham (Gen. 15:1).
2. Moses (Exod. 3:4-10).
3. Joshua (Jos. 1:1-7).
4. Balaam (Num. 22:38).
5. Samuel (1 Sam. 3:4-14).
6. Solomon (1 Kings 3:5-6).
7. David (2 Sam. 2:1).

8. Shemaiah (1 Kings 12:22).
9. The young prophet (1 Kings 13:1).
10. Elijah (1 Kings 17:24).
11. Jonah (Jonah 1:1-2).
12. Nathan (1 Chro. 17:3-4).
13. Isaiah (Isa. 7:3).
14. Jeremiah (Jer. 43:1).
15. Ezekiel (Ezek. 25:1-3).
16. The Israelites in the wilderness (Acts 10:36; Exod. 19:9).
17. John the Baptist (Luke 3:2).
18. Peter (Luke 5:1-4).19. The Apostles of Christ (Acts 6:7).
20. The Samaritans (Acts 8:14).
21. The Gentiles in Judea (Acts 11:1).
22. Sergius Paulus (Acts 13:7).
23. The Thessalonians (1 Thess. 2:13).
24. The whole world (Matt. 3:17).

WHAT ARE FALSE VOICES?

1. Voices that mislead or seduce (Gen. 3:1-10).
2. Voice of temptation (Matt. 4:10).
3. Voices of evil spirits confessing the truth (Act.16:17).

4. Voices of false prophets or prophets that God did not send (Jer 28:12-17, 14:15).
5. The voice of self (Gal. 6:3-4).
6. Voice of prophets speaking from own hearts (Jer. 14:14-15, 1 Kg. 13:11-29).
7. Voices of prophets speaking what the people want to hear (Isaiah 30:10).
8. Voices of commercial prophets or those hungry for gain (Acts 8:9-23).
9. Voices of prophets under the influence of lying Spirits (1 Kings 22:1-23).
10. Voices of miserable comforters who judge and condemn instead of encouraging.
11. Voices of mockery like those of Michal, Sambalat and Tobia (2 Sam. 6:20, Neh. 6:12).
12. Voices of the oppressors and persecutors, like Goliath for example (1 Sam. 17:1-23).
13. The voice of ignorance (Matt. 12:22-24).
14. Voices of flatterers or soothsayers and hero worshippers (Prov. 26:28, 29:5, 20:19). 126:8-9).
21. False doctrines or doctrines of the devil (1 Tim. 4:1).
22. False voices are generally an instrument of satan to counter the voice of God in a man's life. The Proverbs calls it an enticing words of familiar friends (Prov. 1:10). The good Shepherd leads us through His word and Spirit, but the false voices are fashioned to lead against the words of eternal life or cause men to look back

CHARACTERISTICS AND SIGNS OF FALSE VOICES:

1. Deceptive, being deceived or self deceiving (Act 13:10, Jer. 9:6).
2. Leads to confusion, uncertainty, worry, irritation, anger and condemnation (Job. 22:1-5).
3. Feeling of rejection and fear, even after a divine encounter (1 Kings 19:1-18).
4. Slippery success, renewed aggression or evil trade by barter.
5. Frustration, endless pursuit, perpetual and incurable spiritual illness (James 4:3, Jer. 15:15).
6. Spiritual and physical backwardness (Jer. 7:24).
7. Promises and high hopes that fail (Jer. 8:15).

What kind of voice is leading your life? If your experience in life cannot match the Word of God or your experience in life is making you lose hope in Him who created you and died for you, then clear your ears, you may be hearing the wrong voice.

AGENTS AND SOURCES OF FALSE VOICES

1. Satan, his workers or agents and his victims (Mat. 4:1-10, 1 Sam. 28:1-8).
2. The world or the corporate man and his inventions (Rom. 12:2).

3. The flesh through its indispensable appetites, feelings and reactions (Gal.5:19-21).

4. The individual man and his imagination (Jer. 7:24).

THE ARMOUR AGAINST FALSE VOICES

1. You must be dead to sin, the world and the flesh, and be alive to God through Jesus Christ (Rm 6:1-11).

2. You must be filled with the Holy Spirit, not just attending a firebrand church. There is no corporate anointing for salvation (Acts 2:38).

3. Do not be delivered to do abomination (Jer. 7:8-11).

4. Hunger and thirst after righteousness through the Word of God (Mat. 5:6).

5. Pray and fast in hope of eternal life through our Lord Jesus Christ (Rm. 2:7).

6. Be addicted to obedience, even when it hurts (1 Sam. 15:22).

7. Put on the whole armour of God. (Eph. 6:11-18).

If you have the Holy Spirit on the inside, you can stand any kind of battle on the outside

Bible
STUDY
2

THE
HOLY SPIRIT?

WHO IS THE HOLY SPIRIT?

MEMORY VERSE:
Zech. 4:6: "Then he answered and spake unto me, saying, This is the word of the Lord unto Zerubbabel, saying, Not by might, nor by power, but by my spirit, saith the Lord of Hosts.

TEXT: Acts 2

INTRODUCTION These series of studies are going to be some of the most important Bible studies you have ever had. This is because of the importance of the Holy Spirit in the life of the believer. There is a lot of ignorance amongst believers regarding the personality, the activities and the role of the Holy Spirit in the life of a Christian. When thoroughly understood in the context of these teachings, the spiritual poverty will be eliminated forever.

IMPORTANT TRUTHS ABOUT THE HOLY SPIRIT

1. The Christian's heart is the Holy Spirit's home.
2. Unless we have within us that which is above us, we soon shall yield to the pressures around us.
3. If you have the Holy Spirit on the inside, you can withstand any kind of battle on the outside.
4. Christ departed, so that the Holy Spirit could be imparted.
5. The human spirit fails, unless the Holy Spirit fills.
6. You cannot drink of the Holy Spirit on Sunday and the spirits of the world during the week.
7. The Holy Spirit can do more in a minute than what we can do for ourselves in a lifetime.
8. He, who has the Holy Spirit in his heart and the Scripture in his hands, has all he needs.
9. The Holy Spirit is God at work.

10. To build temples is easier than to be temples of the Holy Spirit.

11. One taught by the Spirit knows the will of God.

12. Without the Holy Spirit, the preacher is as helpless before a sinner needing a Saviour, as Samson before Delilah.

WHO IS THE HOLY SPIRIT?

1. Holy Spirit is the executor of the Trinity.
2. The Holy Spirit is God's executive agent in the world today.
3. The Holy Spirit is the bridge to God within you.
4. The Holy Spirit is the voice of God instilled within His children.
5. The Holy Spirit is the constant resource and companion.

6. The Holy Spirit is God.
7. The Holy Spirit is a Person with a mind, emotions and will.
8. The Holy Spirit is God present with us and active amongst us.
9. The Holy Spirit is God around us in everyday experience.
10. The Holy Spirit is part of the Trinity, whom Jesus promised would come to be our Counsellor (John 14:6).
11. The Holy Spirit is the Spirit of the Father.
12. The Holy Spirit is the Spirit of Jesus Christ.
13. The Holy Spirit is the Creator and Giver of life (Job 33:4).
14. The Holy Spirit is the director of ministers (Acts 8:29; 16:6,7).
15. The Holy Spirit is the instructor of ministers (1 Cor. 2:13).
16. The Holy Spirit is the one who speaks in and by the prophets (Acts 1:16).
17. The Holy Spirit is the one who strives with sinners (Gen. 6:3).
18. The Holy Spirit is the one who reproves (John 16:8).
19. The Holy Spirit is the Comforter (Acts 9:31).
20. The Holy Spirit is the helper of our infirmities (Rom. 8:26).
21. The Holy Spirit is the teacher (John 14:26; 1 Cor. 12:3).

22. The Holy Spirit is the one who guides (John 16:13).
23. The Holy Spirit is the one who sanctifies (Rom. 15:16).
24. The Holy Spirit is the one who testifies of Christ (John 15:26).
25. The Holy Spirit is the one who glorifies Christ (John 16:14).
26. The Holy Spirit is the one who searches all things (Rom. 11:33).
27. The Holy Spirit is the one who dwells with the saints (John 14:17).
28. The Holy Spirit is the one who inspires the writing of the Scriptures (2 Sam. 23:2).

29. The Holy Spirit is the one present at work in creation (Gen. 1:2).
30. The Holy Spirit is the one who came upon Joseph in (Gen. 41:38).
31. The Holy Spirit is the one who came upon Moses in (Num. 11:17).
32. The Holy Spirit is the one who came upon Joshua in (Num. 27:18).
33. The Holy Spirit is the one who came upon Othniel in (Judges 3:10).
34. The Holy Spirit is the one who came upon Gideon in (Judges 6:34).
35. The Holy Spirit is the one who came upon Jephthah in (Judges 11:29).
36. The Holy Spirit is the one who came upon Samson in (Judges 14:6, 19).
37. The Holy Spirit is the one who came upon Saul in (1 Sam. 10:10).
38. The Holy Spirit is the one who came upon David in (1 Sam. 16:13).
39. The Holy Spirit is the one who came upon Elijah in (1 Kings 18:12).
40. The Holy Spirit is the one who came upon Elisha in (2 Kings 2:15).
41. The Holy Spirit is the one who came upon Zechariah the high priest in (2 Chron. 24:20).
42. The Holy Spirit is the one who came upon Israel's elders in (Number 11:25).

43. The Holy Spirit is the one who led Israel through the wilderness (Neh. 9:20).
44. The Holy Spirit is the one who will minister to Israel during the millennial reign (Zech. 12:10; Ezek. 37:13-14).
45. The Holy Spirit is the one who restrains the power of satan (2 Thessa. 2:7-14).
46. The Holy Spirit is the one who provided the Saviour with His earthly body (Luke 1:35; Matt. 1:18-20).
47. The Holy Spirit is the anointed Saviour (Matt. 3:16; Luke 4:18; Acts 10:38; Heb. 1:9).
48. The Holy Spirit is the one who directed the Saviour to be tempted by satan (Mat. 4:1).
49. The Holy Spirit is the one who empowered the Saviour (Matt. 12:28).
50. The Holy Spirit is the one who caused the Saviour to sorrow (John 11:33).
51. The Holy Spirit is the one who caused the Saviour to rejoice (Luke 10:21).
52. The Holy Spirit is the one who led the Saviour to Calvary (Heb. 9:14).
53. The Holy Spirit is the one who raised the body of the Saviour (Rom. 8:11).
54. The Holy Spirit is the one who convicts the unsaved person of sin, righteousness and judgement (Acts 2:1-4).
55. The Holy Spirit is the one who gave birth to the church (Acts 2:1-4).

56. The Holy Spirit is the who inspires the worship service of the church (Phil 3:3).
57. The Holy Spirit is the one who directs the church missionary works (Acts 8:29).
58. The Holy Spirit is the one who aids the church singing service (Eph. 5:18-19).
59. The Holy Spirit is the one who appoints the church preachers (Acts 20:28).
60. The Holy Spirit is the one who anoints the church preachers (1 Cor. 2:4).
61. The Holy Spirit is the one who warns church members (1 Tim. 4:1).
62. The Holy Spirit is the one who determines the church decisions (Acts 15:28).
63. The Holy Spirit is the one who directs the church evangelistic attempts (Rev. 22:17).
64. The Holy Spirit is the one who is able to condone or condemn the church (Rev. 2:7).
65. The Holy Spirit is the one who regenerates the believing sinner (Tit. 3:5).
66. The Holy Spirit is the one who baptises the believers (Rom. 6:3-4).
67. The Holy Spirit is the one who indwells the believers (John 14:16).
68. The Holy Spirit is the one who seals the believers (2 Cor. 1:22).
69. The Holy Spirit is the one who fills the believer (Acts 2:4).

70. The Holy Spirit is the one who conforms believers to the image of Christ (2 Cor. 3:18).
71. The Holy Spirit is the one who strengthens the believers' new nature (Eph. 3:16).
72. The Holy Spirit is the one who reveals biblical truths to believers (1 Cor. 2:10).
73. The Holy Spirit is the one who assures believers concerning salvation and service (Rom. 8:16).
74. The Holy Spirit is the one who gives believers liberty (Rom. 8:2).
75. The Holy Spirit is the one who fills the mouth of believers with appropriate things (Mark 3:11).
76. The Holy Spirit is the one who prays for believers (Rom. 8:26).
77. The Holy Spirit is the one who guides believers (John 16:13).
78. The Holy Spirit is the one who teaches believers (1 John 2:27).
79. The Holy Spirit is the one who empowers believers for witnessing (Acts 1:8).
80. The Holy Spirit is the one who imparts the love of Christ to believers, and through the believers (Rom. 5:5).
81. The Holy Spirit is the one who will someday raise the bodies of all departed believers (Rom. 8:11).

Bible
S T U D Y
3

SPIRITUAL POWER?

WHAT IS SPIRITUAL POWER?

MEMORY VERSE

Psalm 62:11: "God hath spoken once; twice have I heard this; that power belongeth unto God."

TEXT Acts 1

INTRODUCTION It is becoming increasingly clear, that 'ice-cream' Christianity, laziness, slumbering prayers and low-spiritual energy will not get us anywhere. It is tragic to note that our current generation is a powerless one. In many situations, the judge has become the accused, and the servants have taken over the horses of the masters.

One of the greatest needs of today's church is bringing down the power of God. We need to demonstrate to this dying unbelieving world, that there can still be signs and wonders which convince people that, with God, nothing is impossible. We need to show to the world the manifestation of the kingdom of God to destroy the works of the devil. We need to turn the world upside down, by displaying the raw power of God. We need to display the supernatural power to solve human problems. We need to heal the sick, cleanse the lepers, raise the dead, cast out demons and bring salvation and deliverance to souls in satanic bondage.

More than at any other time, we need to bring down the fire power of God against the enemy. Why do we need to bring down the power of God? Demonic activities are in a terrible rage. Sins, sicknesses, diseases, curses, and untold problems are mounting and increasing daily. There are a lot of sufferings, poverty and lack in the world. Occult and satanic powers are nakedly displaying their powers. We therefore cannot afford to be powerless in the face of these assaults. It is an insult on your salvation for Pentecostal witchcraft, hypnotism, magic, voodoo, charms and fetish powers, to prosper in the life of a child of God.

Although there is restlessness and pressure mounted upon many for moving forward, many find it impossible to enter into the school of power. While evil men are waxing stronger and stronger, our powerlessness is becoming legendary.

WHAT IS POWER?

Power is an interesting word to define. The difficulty in defining power leads man to classify the different powers as ways of defining it. Powers are therefore classified into: solar power, physical power, technological power, spiritual power, material power, economic power, cultural power, political power, military power. Some even talk of bottom power, money power, magical power, mystical power, etc. There are also such satanic powers as fetish power, juju power, ogbanje power, babalawo power, etc. When men define power, they are talking about:

1. Ability to do or act.
2. Capability of doing or accomplishing something.
3. Political or economic strength.
4. The person or thing that possesses or exercises authority or influence.
5. A military force.
6. Vital energy to make choices and decisions.
7. Capacity to overcome.
8. A specific capacity.
9. Other capacities: to speak, convince, argue, charm, mesmerise, cause trouble, etc.
10. Power is the faculty or capacity to act effectively.
11. Forcefulness.
12. Ability to exercise control.
13. Strength or force exerted or capable of being exerted.
14. Applied force.
15. Intensity.
16. Mechanical energy.
17. Might.
18. Muscle.
19. Omnipotence.
20. Potency.
21. Potential.
22. Competence.
23. Dynamism.
24. Effectiveness.

25. Efficacy.
26. Endowment.
27. Faculty.
28. Function.
29. Influence.
30. Potentiality.
31. Qualification.
32. Skill.
33. Talent.
34. Virtue

WHAT IS SPIRITUAL POWER?

Power is like beauty. If you have to tell people that you are beautiful, then you are not. The only language the enemy respects is the language of power. The Bible is the only book that describes power accurately. The Bible makes us to understand that God is the ultimate source of power (Heb 4:12; Rom. 1:16; 1 Cor. 1:18; James 5:16-18; Rev. 12:11; Acts 1:8; Philp 3:10) and identifies power with the following characteristics:

1. The fullness of Christ dwelling in you (Col. 2:9).
2. Ability to go extra mile (Matt. 5:41).
3. Ability to turn the left cheek (Luke 6:29).
4. Ability to love those who do not love you (Matt. 5:44).
5. Ability to act and not react, when you are offended.
6. Being endued you with the capability to die and for Christ to reign in you (Gal. 2:20).

7. Being worthy, for the Lord to depend on you anywhere you are (Job 1:8).
8. The ability to remain unpolluted by the present world (Heb. 12:1).
9. Having access to the secrets or mysteries of God and remove obstacles in your way (Amos 3:7).
10. Ability to keep your flesh under control (1 Cor. 9:27).
11. Ability to be silent in the face of provocation (Isa. 53:7).
12. Being filled with the Holy Spirit (Acts 1:8).
13. Power to put your enemy to flight (Deut. 28:7).
14. Ability to remove obstacles in your way (Matt. 17:20).
15. Ability to move in supernatural gifts (1 Cor. 12).
16. Being truly broken (John 12:24).

DIFFERENCES BETWEEN POWER AND AUTHORITY:

1. Authority comes from the Word of God, that is, what God has said (Psalm 138:2).
2. Power comes from the anointing of the Holy Spirit (Acts 1:8).
3. Authority is exercised in the name of Jesus (Phil 2:9-10).
4. Power is operated by the anointing (Isa. 10:27; Acts 10:38).
5. Authority is given to every Christian without measure (Mark 16:17).

6. Power is given, according to self-crucifixion and faith (Gal. 2:20; 1 Cor. 15:31).
7. Authority is received by being born again (John 3:3).
8. Power is by living and moving in the realm of the spirit (1 Cor. 12).
9. Authority expresses your legal right as a Christian (Rom 6).
10. Power enforces your legal right as a Christian (Acts 16).
11. Authority is useless without power to punish.
12. Authority without power is a disaster.

Prayer
WATCH
1

6:00 AM

PRAYER WATCH 1
6:00AM

Confessions:

Galatians 3:13-14: Christ hath redeemed us from the curse of the law, being made a curse for us: for it is written, Cursed is every one that hangeth on a tree: That the blessing of Abraham might come on the Gentiles through Jesus Christ; that we might receive the promise of the Spirit through faith.

2 Tim. 4:18: And the Lord shall deliver me from every evil work, and will preserve me unto his heavenly kingdom: to whom be glory for ever and ever. Amen.

Col. 1:13: Who hath delivered us from the power of darkness, and hath translated us into the kingdom of his dear Son:

Col. 2:15: And having spoiled principalities and powers, he made a shew of them openly, triumphing over them in it.

Praise Worship

Prayer Points:

1. Father, I praise Your Holy Name for bearing my burdens on daily basis.
2. O God, I thank You for You are the Refiner.
3. O God, I thank You for the greatness of Your works.
4. O God, I thank You for You are the Sun of Righteousness.
5. O God, I thank You for You are a great God and King over all gods.
6. My Father, I thank You for being my Physician.
7. Great Father of Glory, I thank You because in Your hands are the depths of the earth, and the mountain peaks belong to You.
8. My Father, I thank You for You are my Messiah.
9. O God, I thank You for the marvelous things that You have done for me.
10. Father, thank You for being my Prophet.

> O God, I thank You for You are a great God and King over all gods.

11. O God, I thank You for redeeming my life from the pit and for crowning me with compassion and love.
12. O Lord, I thank You for being the Strength of my soul.
13. O God, I thank You for satisfying my desires with good things, so that my strength is renewed like the eagle's.
14. O God, I thank You for being my Cornerstone.
15. Father, I thank You for making the cloud Your chariots and for riding on the wings of the wind.
16. Father, You are praised for being the Great High Priest.
17. Father, glory be to Your Holy Name for making the winds Your messengers and Your ministers flames of fire.
18. My Father, I thank You, for being the Bishop of my Soul.
19. O God, I thank You, for You setting the earth on its foundation and it can never be moved.
20. O God, I thank You for You are the God of all grace.
21. O God, I thank You for great are Your works, pondered on by all who delight in them.
22. Holy Spirit, come down upon me and incubate my life afresh, in the name of Jesus.
23. Every anti-repentance spirit in my life, I bind you and cast you out now, in the name of Jesus.
24. Let my steps be withdrawn from every wickedness, in the name of Jesus.
25. I refuse to become a companion of sin, in the name of Jesus.

> O God, I thank You for redeeming my life from the pit and for crowning me with compassion and love.

Deliverance Through The Watches

26. My Father, empty me of selfishness, in the name of Jesus.
27. O Lord, heal every area of backsliding in my spiritual life, in the name of Jesus.
28. O Lord, restore unto me the joy of salvation, in the name of Jesus.
29. O Lord, anoint my head with fresh oil, in the name of Jesus.
30. My Father, cast me not away from thy presence, in the name of Jesus.
31. Blessed Holy Spirit, break and mould me after You, in the name of Jesus.
32. Plant my heart, O Lord, in Your ways, and create a deep hunger for You in my heart, in the name of Jesus.
33. Holy Ghost, show me where I have fallen, and make me to do the first works, in the name of Jesus.
34. Jesus, remove not my candlestick from Your presence, in the name of Jesus.
35. O Lord, let no one defile me any more, in the name of Jesus.
36. Lord God Almighty, visit me afresh and let Your light shine upon me once again, in the name of Jesus.
37. Holy Ghost, quicken me and bring me alive, in the name of Jesus.
38. O Lord, subdue in me, the love of sin, in the name of Jesus.
39. O Lord, renovate my life for Your use, in the name of Jesus.

40. O Lord, break the pride in me to pieces and scatter it to the winds, in the name of Jesus.
41. Empower me, O Lord, to walk by Your side, in the name of Jesus.
42. O Lord, create in me a clean heart by Your power and renew a right spirit within me, in the name of Jesus.
43. O Lord, teach me to die to self.
44. O Lord, establish me as a holy person unto You.
45. O Lord, restore my spiritual eyes and ears in the name of Jesus.
46. O Lord, produce in me the power of self-control and gentleness.
47. O Lord, let the anointing of the Holy Spirit break every yoke of backwardness in my life.
48. Let every rebellion flee from my heart, in the name of Jesus.
49. I command every spiritual contamination in my life to receive cleansing by the Blood of Jesus.
50. Let the brush of the Lord scrub out every dirtiness in my spiritual pipe, in the name of Jesus.

> O Lord, let the anointing of the Holy Spirit break every yoke of backwardness in my life.

Prayer
WATCH
2

9:00AM

PRAYER WATCH 2
9:00AM

Confessions:
Numbers 23:23: Surely there is no enchantment against Jacob, neither is there any divination against Israel: according to this time it shall be said of Jacob and of Israel, What hath **God wrought**!

Praise Worship

Prayer Points:

1. Thank God for being the God that answers prayers.
2. Confess every known sin in your life and ask for the mercy of God.
3. Cover yourself with the Blood of Jesus.
4. Every word, vision and dream that did not originate from the Holy Spirit, I render you null and void, in the name of Jesus.

5. Every tree that God the Father has not planted in my life, be uprooted by fire, in the name of Jesus.
6. Every power of darkness, assigned against my life, die, in the name of Jesus.
7. I use the Blood of Jesus to insulate my spirit and soul from all demonic influences, in the name of Jesus.
8. Every power of darkness using my dreams to manipulate my life, die, in the name of Jesus.
9. Let the angels of God gather heavenly resources to fight all my adversaries, in the name of Jesus.
10. Every evil spirit that has attacked me in the dream, die, in the name of Jesus.
11. Every evil prophecy and negative pronouncement over my life, be cancelled by the power in the Blood of Jesus.
12. I renounce every familiar spirit, and I reject their covenants, in the name of Jesus.
13. Every spirit of death and grave, loose your hold upon my life, in the name of Jesus.
14. Every curse of untimely death upon my life, break, by the Blood of Jesus, in the name of Jesus.
15. Every agent of the spirit of death assigned against my life, be arrested, in the name of Jesus.
16. Every harassment of the spirit of death in my dreams, die, in the name of Jesus.
17. Every arrow of death and destruction, go back to your senders, in the name of Jesus.
18. I shall not die, I shall live long, the number of my days shall be fulfilled to declare the works of God, in the name of Jesus.

> Every power of darkness using my dreams to manipulate my life, die, in the name of Jesus.

19. Every coffin prepared for my life, catch your owner, in the name of Jesus.
20. Every satanic funeral procession organised against me, scatter, in the name of Jesus.
21. Every satanic poison in my body, melt away by the Blood of Jesus.
22. Every arrow of pain and sickness, go back to your sender, in the name of Jesus.
23. Every arrow of weakness and disease, go back to your sender, in the name of Jesus.
24. Every arrow of insanity and suffering, go back to your sender, in the name of Jesus
25. My body, eject every satanic poison, in the name of Jesus.
26. Every disease planted into my body through dreams, come out and die, in the name of Jesus.
27. Every spiritual poison in my body, I eject you by the Blood of Jesus, in the name of Jesus.

28. Every effort of the enemy to weaken my prayer altar, be frustrated, in the name of Jesus.
29. Every unclean spirit assigned to be polluting my body in the dreams, die, in the name of Jesus.
30. Every spirit spouse assigned to be molesting me in the dreams, die, in the name of Jesus.
31. Let the thunder and the lightning of God blind every spirit spouse, in the name of Jesus.
32. Every spirit of immorality, wickedness and witchcraft manifesting in form of dogs and serpents in my dreams, die, in the name of Jesus.
33. I barricade my life and home with the fire of God against the operations of spirit spouses, in Jesus' name.
34. Every remains from spirit spouse in my body, be flushed out by the Blood of Jesus, in the name of Jesus.
35. Every dream of backwardness, die, in the name of Jesus.
36. Every power using my dreams to hold back my progress in life, die, in the name of Jesus.
37. Every garment of backwardness, I reject you, catch fire, in the name of Jesus.
38. I bind and cast out every spirit of limitation, in the name of Jesus.
39. Every satanic clothe of non-achievement, you are not my portion, I reject you, catch fire, in Jesus' name.
40. Every gathering where my downfall is being discussed, arrow of fire, scatter them, in the name of Jesus.

41. Every satanic verdict of demotion for my life, be cancelled by the Blood of Jesus, in the name of Jesus.
42. All the blessings the Lord has given unto me shall remain with me for life, in the name of Jesus.
43. In every area of life, I shall not be demoted, in the name of Jesus.
44. This year, shame shall not know my life and my habitation, in the name of Jesus.
45. Every known and unknown covenant of water spirits for my life, be cancelled by the Blood of Jesus, in the name of Jesus.
46. Every water where I have swam in the dream, dry up by fire, in the name of Jesus.
47. Every spirit that has been oppressing me in the dream, die, in the name of Jesus.
48. Every dream of hopelessness, die, in the name of Jesus.
49. Every senseless and meaningless dream, die, in the name of Jesus.
50. Every negative dream shall not come to pass in my life, in the name of Jesus.
51. Every spiritual cannibal, vomit everything you have eaten from me, in the name of Jesus.
52. Every spirit behind evil dreams in my life, die, in the name of Jesus.
53. Let the finger of God unseat my household strongman, in the name of Jesus.
54. I bind the strongman in my life, and I clear my goods from your possession, in the name of Jesus.

55. You strongman of mind destruction, be bound, in Jesus' name.
56. You strongman of financial destruction, be bound, in Jesus' name.
57. Every strongman of bad luck attached to my life, fall down and die, in Jesus' name.
58. I bind every strongman militating against my home, in the name of Jesus
59. I bind and paralyse every strongman of death and hell, in the name of Jesus.
60. You evil strongman attached to my destiny, be bound, in Jesus' name.
61. Every strongman of my father's house, die, in the name of Jesus.
62. Every strongman assigned by the evil powers of my father's house against my life, die, in the name of Jesus.

> Every soul-tie and covenant between me and my former house, office, school, break and loose your hold, in the name of Jesus.

63. Every strongman assigned to weaken my faith, catch fire, in the name of Jesus.
64. I bind and I render to nothing all the strongmen that are currently troubling my life, in the name of Jesus.
65. Let the backbone of the stubborn pursuer and strongman break, in the name of Jesus.
66. I bind every strongman having my goods in his possessions, in the name of Jesus.
67. I clear my goods from the warehouse of the strongman, in the name of Jesus
68. I withdraw the staff of the office of the strongman delegated against me, in the name of Jesus
69. I bind every strongman delegated to hinder my progress, in the name of Jesus.
70. I bind the strongman behind my spiritual blindness and deafness, and paralyse his operations in my life, in the name of Jesus.
71. Every ancestral covenant affecting my life, break and loose your hold, in the name of Jesus.
72. Every inherited family covenant affecting my life, break and loose your hold, in the name of Jesus.
73. Every inherited covenant affecting my life, break and release me, in the name of Jesus.
74. Any evil covenant prospering in my family, be broken by the Blood of Jesus.
75. Every soul-tie and covenant between me and ancestral spirits break and release me, in the name of Jesus.

76. Every soul-tie and covenant with any dead relations, break now and release me, in the name of Jesus.
77. Every soul-tie and covenant between me and family gods, shrines and spirits, break now and release me, in Jesus' name.
78. Every soul-tie and covenant between me and my parents break and release me, in the name of Jesus.
79. Every soul-tie between me and my grandparents, break and release me, in the name of Jesus.
80. Every soul-tie and covenant between me and former boyfriends or girlfriends, break and loose your hold, in the name of Jesus.
81. Every soul-tie and covenant between me and any spirit husband or wife, break and loose your hold, in Jesus' name.
82. Every soul-tie and covenant between me and any demonic ministers, break and loose your hold, in Jesus' name.
83. Every soul-tie and covenant between me and my former house, office, school, break and loose your hold, in the name of Jesus.
84. Every soul-tie and covenant between me and water spirit, break and loose your hold, in the name of Jesus.
85. Every soul-tie and covenant between me and serpentine spirit, break and loose your hold, in the name of Jesus.
86. Any covenant empowering my household enemy, break and loose your hold, in the name of Jesus.

87. Every soul-tie and covenant between me and any occult relation break, and loose your hold, in Jesus' name.
88. Every soul-tie and covenant between me and any dead relation break and loose your hold, in the name of Jesus.
89. Any evil covenant strengthening the foundation of any bondage, be broken, in the name of Jesus.
90. Every soul-tie and covenant between me and familiar spirit, break and loose your hold, in the name of Jesus.

> Any evil covenant prospering in my family, be broken by the Blood of Jesus.

91. Every soul-tie and covenant between me and spiritual night caterers, break and loose your hold, in Jesus' name.
92. Every soul-tie and covenant between me and any territorial spirit, break and loose your hold, in Jesus' name.
93. Every soul-tie and covenant between me and any demonic church that I have ever attended, break and loose your hold, in the name of Jesus.

94. Every soul-tie and covenant between me and any herbalist, break and loose your hold, in the name of Jesus.
95. Every soul-tie and covenant between me and marine kingdom, break and loose your hold, in the name of Jesus.
96. Every soul-tie and covenant between me and witchcraft spirit, break and loose your hold, in the name of Jesus.
97. Every soul-tie and covenant between me and spirit of barrenness, break and loose your hold, in Jesus' name.
98. Every soul-tie and covenant between me and spirit of poverty, break and loose your hold, in the name of Jesus.
99. Every soul-tie and covenant between me and spirit of infirmity and sickness, break and loose your hold, in the name of Jesus.
100. Every soul-tie and covenant between me and the spirit of insanity, break and loose your hold, in Jesus' name.
101. Every soul-tie and covenant between me and the spirit of backwardness and demotion, break and loose your hold, in the name of Jesus.
102. Every soul-tie and covenant between me and the spirit of failure, break and loose your hold, in Jesus' name.

Prayer
WATCH

3

12:00 PM

PRAYER WATCH 3

12:00 NOON

Confessions:
Obadiah 1:7

Praise Worship

Prayer Points:

1. Thank God for His power to deliver from every bondage.
2. I break myself from every spirit of sexual perversion, in the name of Jesus.
3. I release myself from every spiritual pollution emanating from my past sins of fornication and sexual immorality, in the name of Jesus.
4. I release myself from every ancestral pollution, in the name of Jesus.
5. I release myself from every dream pollution, in the name of Jesus.

> Father Lord, let every demonic stronghold built in my life by the spirit of sexual perversion be pulled down, in the name of Jesus.

| Deliverance Through The Watches | 57

6. I command every evil plantation of sexual perversion in my life to come out with all its roots, in the name of Jesus.
7. Every spirit of sexual perversion, working against my life, be paralysed and get out of my life, in the name of Jesus.
8. Every demon of sexual perversion assigned to my life, be bound, in the name of Jesus.
9. Father Lord, let the power of sexual perversion oppressing my life received the fire of God and be roasted, in the name of Jesus.
10. Every inherited demons of sexual perversion in my life, receive the arrows of fire and remain permanently bound, in the name of Jesus.
11. I command every force of power of sexual perversion to come against themselves, in the name of Jesus.
12. Father Lord, let every demonic stronghold built in my life by the spirit of sexual perversion be pulled down, in the name of Jesus.
13. Let every power of sexual perversion that have summoned my life be shattered to pieces, in the name of Jesus.
14. Let my soul be delivered from the forces of sexual perversion, in the name of Jesus.
15. Let the Lord God of Elijah arise with a strong hand against every spirit wife/husband and power of sexual perversion, in the name of Jesus.
16. I break the hold of any evil power over my life, in the name of Jesus.
17. I nullify every effect of the bite of sexual perversion upon my life, in the name of Jesus.
18. Every evil stranger and satanic deposit in my life, I command you to be paralysed and get out of my life,

in the name of Jesus.
19. Holy Ghost Fire, purge my life completely, in the name of Jesus.
20. I claim my complete deliverance in the name of Jesus from the spirit of fornication and sexual immorality, in the name of Jesus.
21. Let my eyes be delivered from lustfulness, in the name of Jesus.
22. As from today, let my eyes be controlled by the Holy Spirit, in the name of Jesus.
23. Holy Ghost Fire, fall upon my eyes and burn to ashes every evil force and satanic powers controlling my eyes, in the name of Jesus.
24. I move from bondage to liberty in every area of my life, in the name of Jesus.
25. Thank God for answers to your prayers.

Prayer
WATCH
4

3:00PM

PRAYER WATCH 4

3:00PM

PraiseWorship

Prayer Confession:
In the name of Jesus Christ, as I make this confession of the word of God into my life, I believe and I receive the power that is in the Word of God into my spirit, soul and body, in the name of Jesus Christ. Amen.

In my mouth is the power of life and death. I speak life unto myself, and I speak destruction unto all my enemies and all their weapons against me, in Jesus' name. Amen.

With my heart, I believe unto righteousness; and with my mouth, confession is made unto salvation in Jesus' name. Amen.

The name of Jesus is my authority over all the powers of darkness including satan, in Jesus', name. Amen.

As I begin to make this confession, I command that at

the name of Jesus Christ, every knee should bow, of things in heaven, things on earth and things under the earth, in Jesus' name. Amen.

As I speak the Word of God right now, I send it to run swiftly and become operational, to manifest and fulfill the purpose for which I send it, in Jesus' name. Amen.

Right now, I command the word to go forth, in Jesus' name. Amen.

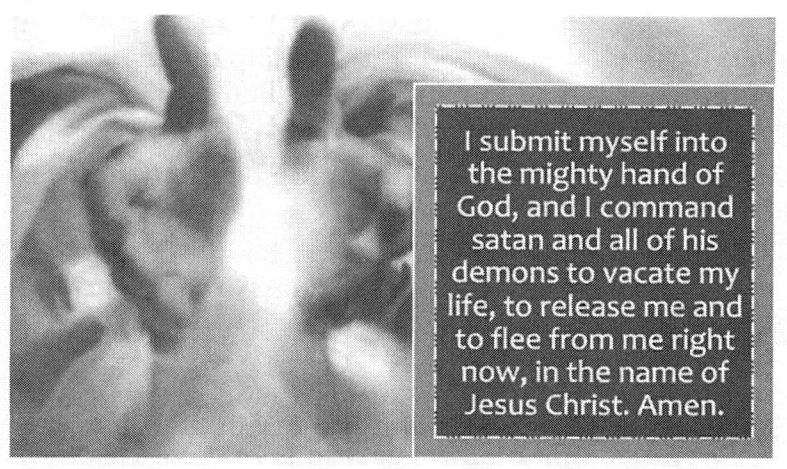

> I submit myself into the mighty hand of God, and I command satan and all of his demons to vacate my life, to release me and to flee from me right now, in the name of Jesus Christ. Amen.

I am a child of God, I believe in the Father, I believe in the Son and I believe in the Holy Ghost, in Jesus' name.

I believe that Jesus Christ came in the flesh and laid down His life, and shed His Blood for me on the cross of Calvary, in Jesus' name. Amen.

I believe that Jesus has defeated satan, and delivered me from this present evil world and satan, in Jesus' name. Amen.

I have accepted Jesus Christ as my personal Saviour, I belong to the Lord Jesus Christ. I am a new creature, old things are passed away; my old life is done away with, I am now living a new life, the life I now live is in Christ Jesus. Jesus Christ has paid the price for me with His Blood and set me free, satan and all his demons have no more power or dominion over my life, in Jesus' name. Amen.

For whomsoever Jesus has set free is free indeed, and I am free indeed, in Jesus' name. Amen.

Jesus has delivered me from all the powers of darkness. I am delivered from principalities, powers, dominions and all the forces of darkness, in the name of Jesus Christ. Amen.

The devil has no more dominion over me, in Jesus' name. Amen.

I submit myself into the mighty hand of God, and I command satan and all of his demons to vacate my life, to release me and to flee from me right now, in the name of Jesus Christ. Amen.

In the name of Jesus Christ, there is no condemnation for those who are in Christ Jesus; there is no condemnation for me, who is in Christ Jesus, in Jesus' name. Amen.

The Spirit of life in Christ Jesus that dwells in the inside of me has delivered me from the law of sin and death including satan, in Jesus' name. Amen.

In the authority of the name of Jesus Christ, I break, damage, destroy and command to be uprooted right now, all covenants, all agreements, all statements, names and requests of any kind, all promises of any kind and all links of any type made with the kingdom of darkness, including everything that the enemy is holding against me. I break them, cast them down, cancel and reject all of them, in Jesus' name. Amen.

Also, I damage any association with the kingdom of darkness done knowingly or unknowingly, whether done in my sleep or when I was awake. I dissociate and separate myself from all of them, in the name of Jesus Christ. Amen.

In the name of Jesus Christ, I command right now a total destruction of all yokes, burdens, fears, oppressions and terrors of any kind, possessions of any kind organized by the enemy against me. I reject and cancel them, in Jesus' name.

I also command the total destruction of all enchantments, witchcraft, divinations, spells, curses, all ordinances and hand writings done by the enemy against me, a child of God, in the name of Jesus Christ. Amen.

I command all these things that I have declared to be destroyed all together, leaving nothing. I break them down, I blot them out with the Blood of Jesus Christ shed for my redemption and I nail them to the cross, in Jesus' name. Amen.

I declare that all the devilish acts of the enemy in my life are erased and finished, in Jesus' name. Amen.

Right now, I break myself loose from all the links with the kingdom of darkness, in Jesus' name. Amen.

All their works against me are now spoilt, wiped away and forgotten forever, in the name of Jesus Christ. Amen.

Jesus Christ has set me free from all the captivity of satan and all his demons, in Jesus' name. Amen.

When Jesus Christ ascended, He led captivity captive. He has broken down the gates of brass; He has cut asunder the bars of iron and delivered me from all

> I command all these things that I have declared to be destroyed all together, leaving nothing. I break them down, I blot them out with the Blood of Jesus Christ shed for my redemption and I nail them to the cross, in Jesus' name. Amen.

the imprisonments of the devil made against me, in Jesus' name.

Jesus has also broken down and scattered all the powers of the enemy used against me, in Jesus' name. Amen.

All power in heaven and on earth is given unto me by Christ Jesus. In the authority of the name of Jesus Christ I have the keys to the kingdom of heaven. Whatsoever I loose on earth, is loosed in heaven. Right now, in Jesus' name, I loose myself from every imprisonment of the devil and his followers, in Jesus' name. Amen.

And whatsoever I bind on earth is bound in heaven. Right now, I bind and I put a stop to all the numerousactivities of the devil organised against me, in Jesus' name. Amen.

I ask for the vengeance of the Lord upon all my enemies: "for vengeance is the Lord's", and so the Lord shall repay them on my behalf.

In the name of Jesus Christ, I pour the wrath of God as water upon all my enemies. I conquer and I lock them all up, for God is for me and no one can rise up or be against me, in Jesus' name. Amen.

Jesus Christ is the fighter of all the battles and attacks waged against me by my enemies, in Jesus' name. Amen.

I do not trust in my own arrow and I do not trust in my own sword. I do not fight for myself. It is not by might, nor by power, but by the Spirit of the Lord, in the name of Jesus Christ. Amen.

In the name of Jesus Christ, I hand over all my battles to the Lord Jesus Christ. The Lord fights for me and I hold my peace, in Jesus' name. Amen.

I am an overcomer through the name of Jesus Christ. I am victorious in all circumstances and situations against me, in the name of Jesus. Amen.

I do not need to fight in this battle or any other battle. I stand still. I put my trust in God and I shall see the salvation of the Lord, in the name of Jesus Christ. Jesus Christ has defeated all my enemies and they are brought down and fallen under my feet, in Jesus' name. Right now, I crush them all to the ground and I command them to begin to lick up the dust of the earth under my feet; for at the name of Jesus, every knee must bow, in Jesus' name. Amen.

God has equipped me and made me a danger and a terror to all my enemies, in Jesus' name. The Lord has sent the fear and the dread of me upon all my enemies, report or information on me shall cause them to fear, tremble and be in anguish over me, in Jesus' name. Amen.

I am a soldier for Christ. I am wearing the whole armour of God, in the name of Jesus Christ. Amen.

The armour of God empowers me to have victory over the principalities, against powers, against rulers of darkness of this world, against spiritual wickedness and against all the powers of darkness and even against satan himself, in Jesus' name. Amen.

I am God's power house. The power of God resides in me, and is manifested on the outside of me in Jesus name. Amen.

The glory of God is as a covering roundabout me, in Jesus' name. In the name of Jesus Christ and at the presence of God in my life, I command the wicked to perish before me and to melt away like wax in the fire. None shall be able to stand before me all the days of my life, in Jesus name. Amen.

I am built up in Christ Jesus. As Jesus is, so am I on the face of this earth in the name of Jesus Christ Amen.

I know who I am in Christ. I am a royal priesthood. I am a holy nation. I am a chosen generation and I am a peculiar person delivered from the kingdom of darkness into the marvellous light of Christ Jesus, in Jesus' name Amen.

I know who I am in Christ, in Jesus' name. Amen. In the name of Jesus Christ all demons, even satan, are subject to me in Jesus' name. Amen. Through the name of Jesus, I push down all my enemies and they cannot hurt me in Jesus' name. Amen.

As I make this confession, I send forth a mighty destruction to scatter, to destroy and break in pieces every gathering or association of my enemies against me, in Jesus name. In the name of Jesus Christ, no plot, devices or counsel of the wicked against me shall stand; and every tongue that shall rise up against me in judgement, I condemn it, in Jesus' name. Amen.

Jesus Christ saves me from all those that rise up against me in Jesus' name, Jesus is my defender. Jesus is my rock. Jesus is my deliverer. Jesus is my strength. Jesus is my fortress and my high tower, in Jesus' name. Amen.

No weapon that is formed against me shall prosper in Jesus' name. Amen.

If the enemy comes against me, the Spirit of the Lord will lift up a standard against them and they cannot pass through in Jesus' name. Amen.

The Lord Jesus Christ has set a bound round about me. There is a strong hedge of protection round about me and a powerful hedge that no demon in hell, including satan, can ever cross to reach me, in Jesus' name. Amen.

I am a child of God. I am dwelling in the secret place of the Most High God, I am protected and covered under the shadow of the wings of Jehovah, in Jesus' name. Amen.

The Word of God is the power of God, and the entrance of the Word of God into my life has brought the light of God into my life; and the darkness cannot comprehend it, in Jesus' name. I send forth this light that is in me as a two-edged sword to destroy all the kingdoms of darkness, in Jesus' name. Amen.

The Word of God is quick and powerful in my mouth. God has put the power of His word in my mouth, in Jesus' name. I trust in the Word of God, the Word stands sure. When I speak it, it will accomplish the purpose for which I have spoken it, in Jesus' name Amen.

Right now, I send the Word of God as a missile to destroy al principalities, powers, thrones, rulers of darkness and all wicked spirits, in Jesus' name. Amen.

I receive the Word of God as a shield and covering over my life, in Jesus' name. Amen.

My God is the God that answers by fire. God has fully armed me with His fire for the destruction of all my enemies, including satan in Jesus' name. Amen.

My body is the temple of the Holy Spirit. The Spirit of God dwells in me, in Jesus' name. Amen.

I am a container for the fire of the Holy Ghost and the power of God resides in me in Jesus' name. Amen.

As I speak the Word of God, I send it to go forth as fuel of unquenchable fire to consume all my enemies to ashes, in the name of Jesus. Amen.

I receive it to encircle and protect me from all my enemies, in Jesus' name. Amen.

I am fireproof to all the enemies' fire and weapons of war targeted against me in Jesus' name. Amen.

I am a danger to the whole kingdom of darkness. I am as a live wire. Anyone that touches or tries to touch me, shall be electrocuted and set ablaze forever in Jesus' name. Amen.

The Word of God says, "Never touch or try to harm a child of God." I am the apple of God's eye. Anyone thatintends or plots evil against me, God shall destroy in Jesus' name. Amen

I believe and I receive the Blood of Jesus Christ that was shed for me on the cross of Calvary. I am redeemed by the Blood of Jesus. Right now, I take of the Blood of Jesus Christ and I use it to set a boundary round about me, in Jesus' name. Amen.

As I speak the Word of God, I send it to go forth as fuel of unquenchable fire to consume all my enemies to ashes, in the name of Jesus. Amen.

I receive the Blood of Jesus Christ upon me and upon my house where I live, in Jesus' name. Amen.

When the enemy sees the Blood, he shall pass over me. The destroyers will not be able to enter my house because of the Blood of Jesus Christ. If my enemies seek me, they shall not be able to find me, for my life is hidden in the Blood of Jesus, in Jesus' name. Amen.

The Blood of Jesus Christ is a covering and hiding place for me from all of my enemies including satan, in Jesus' name. Amen.

The angels of God hearken to the Word of God. They hear and obey the Word of God, because the Word of God is God, speaking to them. As I speak the Word of God out of my mouth, it will go forth to execute the purpose for which I send the Word in Jesus' name. Amen.

I receive the ammunition of angelic guidance and operations in my life right now, in Jesus' name. Amen.

The angels have been ordered by God to take charge of me in all of my ways and I receive them in Jesus' name. They go ahead of me wherever I go, and they go ahead of me in whatever I do. They go forth and make all the crooked ways straight before me, in Jesus' name. Amen.

The angels of God watch over me at daytime and watch over me at nighttime. They make sure that no evil whatsoever befalls me, in Jesus' name. Amen.

Right now, I send the angels to pursue all my enemies and make them like chaff in the wind. I also send a grievous whirlwind to cover them, to destroy them and to cast them to the bottomless pit, in Jesus' name. Amen.

In the name of Jesus Christ, the mighty hand of God is upon my life, upholding and protecting me from all who rise up against me, in Jesus' name. Amen.

Jesus Christ has made His grace available to me. I ask for the grace and I receive it by faith, in Jesus' name. Amen.

So, when I call upon the name of the Lord, He shall stretch forth His mighty hand, lift me up above all my enemies and deliver me from all of them, in Jesus' name. Amen.

In the name of Jesus, I am inscribed in the palm of God's mighty hand. I am neatly tucked away and hidden from all the evil and troubles of this present world, in Jesus' name. Amen.

No one, whomsoever, be they principalities, powers, dominions or all the powers of darkness and even satan himself, can pluck me out of the mighty hand of God, for my God is stronger than all that He created, in Jesus' name. Amen.

I am armed with the shoes of the gospel of the Lord Jesus Christ which is the power of God, and I wear them and use them to trample on all the powers of darkness. I tread on all snakes and scorpions and I destroy them in Jesus' name. Amen.

My feet are like hinds' feet, the appearance of me is as the appearance of horses. So, I run like horses and chariots. I lead, I go forth conquering and I conquer all my enemies. I am more than a conqueror through Christ Jesus, in Jesus' name. Amen.

I move faster than the speed of light, in Jesus' name. Amen.

I pursue my enemies, I overtake them and destroy them, in Jesus' name. Amen.

The Lord has lifted me up and I am seated with Him in heavenly places in Christ Jesus, far above principalities, powers and dominion. The Lord has put all things under my feet. I use my feet to bruise and destroy all my enemies, even satan, in Jesus' name. Amen.

In Jesus' name, anywhere the soles of my feet shall tread upon, the Lord has given unto me, in Jesus' name. Amen.

I tread upon and completely destroy all strongholds, walls, foundations and barriers of the enemy against me, in Jesus' name. Amen. I tread on them with the shoes of the gospel of the Lord Jesus Christ, I make an utter ruin of them all and an utter end of all their possessions, kingdoms, thrones, dominions, palaces, all their entire kingdoms and everything in them, in Jesus' name. Amen.

I erase them all and I make them completely desolate, in Jesus' name. Amen.

My strength is in the Lord Jesus Christ. Jesus is my strength I receive strength from the Lord, in Jesus' name. Amen.

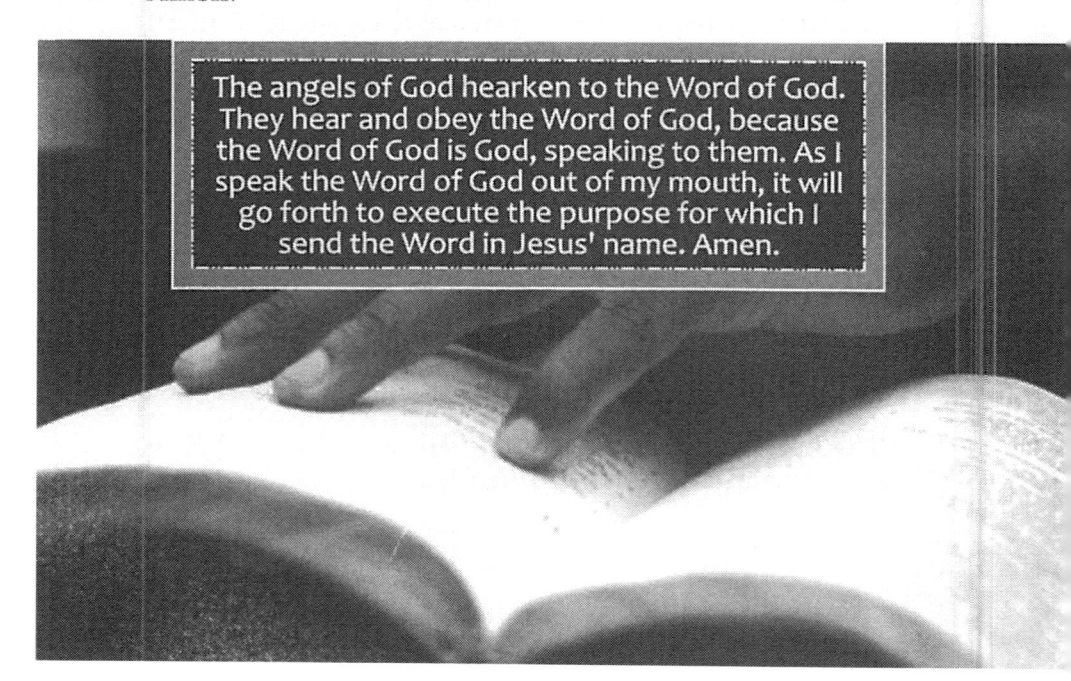

> The angels of God hearken to the Word of God. They hear and obey the Word of God, because the Word of God is God, speaking to them. As I speak the Word of God out of my mouth, it will go forth to execute the purpose for which I send the Word in Jesus' name. Amen.

There is no weakness in me for I have received the might of God. I am strong; I can do all things through Christ who strengthens me. I walk and I do not faint. I run and I am not weary, in Jesus' name. Amen.

The Spirit of Christ that dwells in me strengthens my physical body, in Jesus' name. Amen.

I have prayer power, in Jesus' name. Amen.

I pray without ceasing. I am fortified with strength to pray, in Jesus' name. Amen.

Jesus Christ has given me His peace and I receive it, in Jesus' name. Amen.

I have the peace of God that surpasses all understanding. The peace of God keeps my heart and keeps my mind through Christ Jesus, in Jesus' name. Amen.

My mind is renewed by the Word of God day by day, in Jesus' name. Amen.

My mind is stayed on Christ Jesus. I control my thoughts from thinking evil, in Jesus' name. I cast down every imagination and every high thing that exalts itself against the Word of God in my life and I command my thoughts and mind to be in obedience to Christ, in Jesus' name. Amen.

I am full of faith in God. I do not doubt. I do not operate in unbelief. I believe and trust God as my helper. I do not fear for anything, for God has not given me the spirit of fear. I have the spirit of power and I have a sound mind through Christ, in Jesus' name. Amen.

In the name of Jesus Christ, my body is healed. By the stripes of Jesus Christ, I receive my healing, in Jesus' name. Amen.

Sickness and disease of any kind have no place in my body, in Jesus' name. Jesus has taken all my sicknesses and pains on the cross of Calvary.

And, if I eat or drink any deadly or harmful thing, it cannot hurt me in Jesus' name. Amen.

Right now, in the name of Jesus Christ, I curse every sickness and every disease that have attacked or intend to attack my body, in the name of Jesus; and I command them to die and disappear from my body right now, in the name of Jesus Christ. Amen.

The Spirit of God is a guide for me, in Jesus' name. Amen.

I am led by the spirit. For those who are led by the Spirit of God are the sons of God. Since I acknowledge God as my Father, He will order my footsteps and the Lord will direct my path, in Jesus' name. Amen.

I am not lazy and I am not slack to follow the leadings of the Spirit of God in my life. I am energetic at all times, always yielding and ready to be in obedience to God, in Jesus' name. Amen.

Right now, I reject, I refuse and I bind every voice or leading of the devil, in Jesus' name. Amen.

I repeat: I reject, I refuse and I bind every voice or leading of the devil in my life today and always, in Jesus' name. Amen.

The voice of a stranger I will not hear; the leading of a stranger I will not follow. The Lord is my Shepherd and it

I am not lazy and I am not slack to follow the leadings of the Spirit of God in my life. I am energetic at all times, always yielding and ready to be in obedience to God, in Jesus' name. Amen.

is Him I will hear and it is Him I will follow forever, for Jesus is my Anchor, in Jesus' name. Amen.

Today, right now, as I conclude this confession, I also cancel all negative confessions that I have made at anytime in my life, in Jesus' name. I agree with the will of God for my life. I come against all negative confessions made by me or anyone against me. As I speak, I send the power in the Word of God to change every negative confession to positive, in Jesus' name. Amen.

Against my health, I am healed, in Jesus' name. Amen.

Against my finances, I am rich, I shall lack nothing, in Jesus' name. Amen.

Against my marriage, my marriage is stable; I have peace in my marriage, in Jesus' name. Amen.

Against my children, my children shall prosper in every area and have peace, in Jesus' name. Amen.

Against my calling, what God has purposed in my life must be accomplished, in Jesus' name. Amen.

Against my safety, no accident or evil shall befall me. I do not fear for anything, in Jesus' name. Amen.

Against my life, God has satisfied me with long life in Jesus' name. Amen.

I erase all negative words, all evil statements, all doubtful statements, all unbelief and all other statements that glorify not God, but the devil. I wipe them all off with the Blood of Jesus Christ, in Jesus' name. Amen.

I take control over my speech, in Jesus' name. Amen.

I ask the Lord to help me to set a guard over my lips, in Jesus' name. Amen.

Right now, as I enter into prayer warfare, I submit myself to God completely, in Jesus' name. Amen.

I cast out the devil; I rebuke the devil and I command him to flee from me right now, in the name of Jesus Christ. Amen.

I bind the devil from stealing, killing or destroying anything belonging to me, in Jesus' name, be it in my life or my possession, in Jesus' name. Amen.

As I enter into warfare prayer, I bind the devil and his followers from being a hindrance to my prayers, in Jesus' name. Amen.

I also bind the enemy from throwing any arrow or weapon against me as I pray, in Jesus' name. Amen.

I bind all the enemies' armies and ammunition against me, in Jesus' name. Amen.

The worse things happen in the battle field. But, nothing whatsoever, absolutely nothing will happen to me, in Jesus' name. Amen.

Lord, I ask that all these confessions, that I have made, be operational and be as a covering and a defence over me, over my spirit, soul and body; and all these confessions are to go forth as a destruction to the devil and all my enemies, in Jesus' name. Amen.

As I enter into spiritual warfare, I send the Word of God to damage, destroy and uproot the devil and all his followers, in the name of Jesus Christ. Amen.

Prayer
WATCH
5

6:00 PM

PRAYER WATCH 5
6:00 PM

Confession:

Psalm 68:1: Let God arise, let his enemies be scattered: let them also that hate him flee before him.

Praise Worship:

Prayer Points:

1. O wind of God, drive away every power of the ungodly rising against my destiny, in the name of Jesus.
2. Let the rage of the wicked against me be rendered impotent, in the name of Jesus.
3. Let the imagination of the wicked against me be neutralised, in the name of Jesus.
4. Every counsel of evil kings against me, be scattered, in the name of Jesus.

5. O God, arise and speak in great wrath against the enemy of my breakthroughs, in the name of Jesus.
6. Every band of the wicked that is arresting my progress, break, in the name of Jesus.
7. Every cord of darkness militating against my breakthroughs, die, in the name of Jesus.
8. O God, arise and laugh my enemies to scorn, in Jesus' name.
9. O God, arise and speak unto my enemies in Your wrath, in the name of Jesus.
10. O God, vex my stubborn oppressors in Your sore displeasure, in the name of Jesus.
11. O Lord, break my enemies with Your rod of iron, in Jesus' name.
12. O God, dash the power of my stubborn pursuers in pieces like a potter's vessel, in the name of Jesus.
13. O God, arise with all Your weapons of war and fight my battles for me, in the name of Jesus.
14. O God, be my glory and the lifter of my head, in Jesus' name.
15. My Father, be a shield for me in every situation, in Jesus' name.
16. O God, hear my cry out of Your holy hill, in the name of Jesus.
17. I will not be afraid of ten thousands of people that have set themselves against me, in the name of Jesus.
18. O God, smite my enemies by their cheekbones, in Jesus' name.
19. My Father, break the teeth of the ungodly, in Jesus' name.

20. O Lord, hear my voice whenever I call, in the name of Jesus.

21. O God, visit every power lying against me with destruction, in the name of Jesus.

22. Lead me, O Lord, in Thy righteousness, in the name of Jesus.

23. O Lord, make Your way plain before my face, in Jesus' name.

24. Let my enemies fall by their own counsel, in the name of Jesus.

25 Cast out my enemies in the multitude of their transgressions, in the name of Jesus.

26. Every organised worker of iniquity, depart from me, in the name of Jesus.

27. Let all my enemies be ashamed and sore vexed, in Jesus' name.

28. Let sudden shame be the lot of all my oppressors, in Jesus' name

29. Every power planning to tear my soul like a lion, be dismantled, in the name of Jesus.

> Lead me, O Lord, in thy righteousness, in the name of Jesus.

30. O God, command judgement on all my oppressors, in Jesus' name.
31. Let the wickedness of the wicked come to an end, O Lord, in the name of Jesus.
32. O Lord, let Your anger boil against the wicked every day, in the name of Jesus.
33. O God, prepare the instruments of death against my enemies, in the name of Jesus.
34. O God, ordain Your arrows against my persecutors, in the name of Jesus.
35. Let every pit dug by the enemy for me become a grave for the enemy, in the name of Jesus.
36. Let the mischief of my enemy return upon his own head, in the name of Jesus.
37. Let all weapons of my enemies backfire by thunder, in the name of Jesus.
38. O God, ordain strength for me and silence the enemy and the avenger, in the name of Jesus.
39. When my enemies are turned back, they shall perish out of Thy presence, in the name of Jesus.
40. O God, destroy the wicked and wipe off their names for ever and ever, in the name of Jesus.
41. Let the enemies sink in the pit they have dug for me, in Jesus' name.
42. Let the feet of the enemy be taken in the net in which he has hidden for me, in the name of Jesus.
43. Let the wicked be snared in the work of his own hands, in the name of Jesus.

44. Arise O Lord, let no man prevail against me, let the heathen be judged in Thy sight, in the name of Jesus.

45. Put the enemies in fear, O Lord, that the nations may know themselves to be but men, in the name of Jesus.

46. Let the wicked be taken in the devices that they have imagined, in the name of Jesus.

47. Arise O Lord, lift up Thy arm in war, in the name of Jesus.

48. Break Thou the arm of the wicked and the evil man, in the name of Jesus.

49. Upon the wicked O Lord, rain snares, fire and brimstone and a horrible tempest, in the name of Jesus.

50. My enemies shall not rejoice over me, in the name of Jesus.

51. Keep me as the apple of Thy eye. Hide me under the shadow of Thy wings, O Lord, in the name of Jesus.

52. Barricade me from the wicked that oppress me and from my deadly enemies who compass me about, in the name of Jesus.

53. Arise, O Lord, disappoint my oppressors and cast them down, in the name of Jesus.

54. O Lord, deliver my soul from the wicked, with is Thy sword, in the name of Jesus.

55. I will call upon the Lord, who is worthy to be praised, so shall I be saved from my enemies, in Jesus' name.

56. O God, send out Your arrows and scatter the oppressors, in the name of Jesus.
57. O God, shoot out Your lightening and discomfit them, in the name of Jesus.
58. Let the smoke go out of Your nostrils and fire out of Your mouth to devour all plantations of darkness in my life, in Jesus' name
59. O God, release thunder from heaven against all my oppressors, in the name of Jesus.
60. O Lord, at the blast of Your nostrils, disgrace every foundational bondage in my life, in the name of Jesus.
61. O God, deliver me from my strong enemies who hated me for they are too strong for me, in Jesus' name.
62. O God, bring down every high look that is downgrading my potentials, in the name of Jesus.
63. I receive power to run through satanic troops, in Jesus' name.
64. I receive power to leap over every demonic wall or barrier, in the name of Jesus.
65. O Lord, teach my hands to war, in the name of Jesus.
66. Let every bow of steel fashioned against me by the enemy be broken by my hands, in the name of Jesus.
67. I receive the power to pursue and overtake my enemies, in the name of Jesus.
68. My enemies are wounded. They are unable to rise. they are fallen under my feet, in the name of Jesus.
69. O God, subdue under me those that rose up against me, in the name of Jesus.

70. O God, arise and give me the neck of my enemies so that I might destroy them that hate me, in Jesus' name.
71. My enemies will cry, but there will be none to deliver them, in the name of Jesus.
72. I receive power to beat my aggressors to smallness as the dust before the wind, in the name of Jesus.
73. I cast out my pursuers as the dirt in the street, in Jesus' name.
74. By Your favour, O Lord, the people whom I have not known shall serve me, in the name of Jesus.
75. As soon as they hear of me, they shall obey me. Strangers shall submit themselves unto me, in the name of Jesus.
76. Dark strangers in my life, fade away and be afraid out of your close places, in the name of Jesus.
77. O God, avenge me and subdue my adversaries under me, in the name of Jesus.
78. The Lord shall hear me in the day of trouble. The name of the God of Jacob shall defend me, in the name of Jesus.
79. O Lord, send me help from Your sanctuary and strengthen me out of Zion, in the name of Jesus.
80. My adversaries are brought down and are fallen, but I rise and stand upright, in the name of Jesus.
81. Let Thine hand find out all Thy enemies. Let Thy right hand find out those that hate Thee, in Jesus' name.
82. O God, make my adversaries as a fiery oven in the time of Thine anger, in the name of Jesus.

> Arise O Lord, Let not man prevail, let the heathen be judged in Thy sight, in the name of Jesus.

83. O God, arise and swallow up my enemies in Your wrath and let Your fire devour them, in the name of Jesus.
84. Let every seed and fruit of the enemy fashioned against my destiny be destroyed, in the name of Jesus.
85. Let the mischievous device of the enemy backfire, in the name of Jesus.
86. O God, arise and make all my pursuers turn back, in Jesus' name.
87. O Lord, let Your arrows pursue and locate every wicked power targeted against me, in the name of Jesus.
88. Do not be far from me, O Lord, be my help in the time of trouble, in the name of Jesus.
89. O Lord, make haste to help me, in the name of Jesus.
90. O Lord, deliver my soul from the sword and my destiny from the power of the dog, in the name of Jesus.

91. O God, arise by the thunder of Your power and save me from the lion's mouth, in the name of Jesus.
92. Thou power of the valley of the shadow of death, release my destiny, in the name of Jesus.
93. O gates blocking my blessings, be lifted up, in Jesus' name.
94. O Lord, keep my soul. Let me not be ashamed and deliver me, in the name of Jesus.
95. Every drinker of blood and eater of flesh coming against me, die, in the name of Jesus.
96. Though an host should encamp against me, my heart shall not fear, in the name of Jesus.
97. Though war should rise against me. In this, will I be confident, in the name of Jesus.
98. And now shall my head be lifted up above my enemies round about me, in the name of Jesus.
99. Deliver me not over unto the will of my enemies, in the name of Jesus.
100. God shall destroy the camp of the enemies and their camp shall never be built up, in the name of Jesus.
101. O Lord, according to the deeds of the wicked, give them the works of their hands, in the name of Jesus.
102. O Lord, put off my sack cloth and gird me with gladness, in the name of Jesus.
103. Bow down Thine ear to me, O Lord, and deliver me speedily, in the name of Jesus.
104. Pull me out of the hidden net of the enemy, in Jesus' name.

105. Lord, my times are in Thy hand. Deliver me from the hands of my enemies and from those that persecute me, in the name of Jesus.

106. Let the wicked be ashamed and let them be silent in the grave, in the name of Jesus.

107. Every lying lip speaking against me, be silenced, in Jesus' name.

108. O Lord, bring the counsel of the ungodly to naught, in the name of Jesus.

109. Many sorrows shall be to the wicked, in the name of Jesus.

110. O Lord, make the devices of my adversaries of none effect, in the name of Jesus.

111. Evil shall slay the wicked and they that hate the righteous shall be desolate, in the name of Jesus.

112. Father, fight against them that fight against me, in the name of Jesus.

113. Father, take hold of thy shield and buckler and stand up for my help, in the name of Jesus.

114. Father, draw out Your spear and stop my persecutors, in Jesus' name.

115. Let them be confounded and put to shame that seek after my soul, in the name of Jesus.

116. Let them be turned back and brought to confusion that device my hurt, in the name of Jesus.

117. Let the wicked be as chaff before the wind and let the angel of the Lord chase them, in the name of Jesus.

118. Let the way of the oppressors be dark and slippery and let the angel of the Lord persecute them, in the name of Jesus.

119. Let destruction come upon my enemies unawares and let the nets that they had hidden catch themselves, in Jesus' name.

120. Let the enemy fall into the destruction that he has caused, in the name of Jesus.

121. Let not them that are my enemies wrongfully rejoice over me, in the name of Jesus.

122. Let my enemies be ashamed and be brought to confusion together with them that rejoice at my hurt, in the name of Jesus.

123. Let my enemies be clothed with shame, in the name of Jesus.

124. Stir up Thine self, O Lord; and fight for me, in Jesus' name.

125. Let them be clothed with shame and dishonour that magnify themselves against me, in the name of Jesus.

126. Let not the foot of pride come against me, in Jesus' name.

127. Let not the hand of the wicked prosper in my life, in the name of Jesus.

128. Every worker of death, be cast down and be unable to rise, in the name of Jesus.

129. O God, arise and laugh at the plot of the wicked fashioned against me, in the name of Jesus.

The dark strangers in my life shall fade away and be afraid out of their close places, in the name of Jesus.

130. Let their sword enter into their hearts and let their bows be broken, in the name of Jesus.//
131. Let the arms of the wicked be broken, in the name of Jesus.
132. My enemies shall be as the fat of lambs; they shall be consumed like smoke, in the name of Jesus.
133. Let them be desolate that laugh me to scorn, in Jesus' name.
134. Every enemy saying: "where is my God?", be disgraced, in the name of Jesus.
135. Through Thee, I will push down my enemies, through Thy name, I will tread them under that rise up against me, in Jesus' name.
136. O Lord, break the lips of my Goliath with Your east wind, in the name of Jesus.
137. Let death feed upon every witchcraft power, in Jesus' name.
138. O Lord, redeem my soul from the power of the grave, in the name of Jesus.
139. I will call upon the Lord in the day of trouble and He shall deliver me, in the name of Jesus.
140. Lord, reward evil unto my enemies and cut them off in Thy truth, in the name of Jesus.
141. Destroy, O Lord, and divide every power conspiring against my destiny, in the name of Jesus.
142. Every power of the night working against my victory, die, in the name of Jesus.

143. O Lord, let death seize upon them and let them go down quick to hell that devise disgrace against me, in the name of Jesus.

144. O God, arise and afflict my affliction, in the name of Jesus.

145. When I cry unto Thee, then shall my enemies turn back. This, I know, for God is with me, in the name of Jesus.

146. O God, break the teeth of the evil lion targeted against me, in the name of Jesus.

147. Let my oppressors melt away as waters which run continuously, in the name of Jesus.

148. Let Your whirlwind blow away every oppression, in Jesus' name.

149. Deliver me from the workers of iniquity and save me from bloody men, in the name of Jesus.

150. Every power of the dog working late at night against me, be dismantled, in the name of Jesus.

151. God shall let me see my desires upon my enemies, in the name of Jesus.

152. Scatter them by Your power, O Lord, they that devise my fall, in the name of Jesus.

153. Let my enemies be taken in their pride, in the name of Jesus.

154. Give me help from troubles, for vain is the help of man, in the name of Jesus.

155. Through God, I shall do valiantly, for He shall tread down my enemies, in the name of Jesus.

156. Those that seek my soul to destroy it, shall go down into the lower parts of the earth, in the name of Jesus.

157. My problem shall die by the sword and shall be a portion for foxes, in the name of Jesus.

158. Hear my voice, O God, preserve me from the fear of the enemy, in the name of Jesus.

159. Hide me, O God, from the secret counsel of the wicked, in the name of Jesus.

160. O God, shoot at my enemies with an arrow; suddenly shall they be wounded, in the name of Jesus.

161. The tongue of my adversaries shall fall upon them and all that see them shall flee away, in the name of Jesus.

162. Let God arise and let all His enemies be scattered, let them that hate Him flee before Him, in the name of Jesus.

163. As smoke is driven away, so drive away the hand of the oppressor, in the name of Jesus.

164. Let every power rebelling against my breakthroughs be made to dwell in a dry land, in the name of Jesus.

165. O God, wound the hearts of all my stubborn pursuers, in the name of Jesus.

166. O Lord, rebuke the company of darkness and scatter them, in the name of Jesus.

167. Let the table of my enemies become a snare before them and that which should have been for their welfare, let it become a trap, in the name of Jesus.
168. Pour out Thine indignation upon the enemies of my soul, in the name of Jesus.
169. Let their habitation or house become desolate and let none dwell in their tents, in the name of Jesus.
170. Let those that seek my soul be turned back and put to confusion, in the name of Jesus.
171. Let them be confounded and consumed that are adversaries of my soul, in the name of Jesus.
172. All my enemies shall lick the dust, in the name of Jesus.
173. O God, break the head of the dragon in the waters, in the name of Jesus.
174. O God, break the head of leviathan in pieces, in Jesus' name.
175. Arise, O God, plead Thine own cause, remember how the foolish man reproacheth Thee daily, in the name of Jesus.
176. All the horns of the wicked also shall be cut off, in the name of Jesus.
177. At Thy rebuke, O God of Jacob, both the chariot and the horse are cast into a deep sleep, in the name of Jesus.
178. Let the wrath of the enemy against me be converted to testimonies, in the name of Jesus.
179. O Lord, send evil angels after the enemies of my soul, in the name of Jesus.

180. O God, smite the enemies in their hidden parts and put them to a perpetual reproach, in the name of Jesus.

181. O Lord, feed my enemies with the bread of tears and give them tears to drink in a great measure, in the name of Jesus.

182. Let the stars fight against my enemies after the order of Sisera, in the name of Jesus.

183. O God, make my enemies like a wheel, as the stubble before the wind, in the name of Jesus.

184. Persecute my enemies with Thy tempest and make them afraid with Thy storm, in the name of Jesus.

185. Cover the faces of my aggressors with shame that they may seek thy name, O Lord, in the name of Jesus.

186. Let my enemies be confounded and be troubled, in Jesus' name.

187. All the assembly of the violent men, be scattered, in the name of Jesus.

188. O Lord, break down the hedges of the wicked and bring their strongholds to ruin, in the name of Jesus.

189. I shall not be afraid for the terror by night, nor for the arrow that flieth by day, in the name of Jesus.

190. A thousand shall fall at my side and ten thousand at my right hand, but they shall not come near me, in the name of Jesus.

191. My eyes shall see my desires on my enemies, in Jesus' name

192. Let fire go before me and burn up my enemies round about, in the name of Jesus.
193. At Thy rebuke, let Thine enemies flee. At the voice of Thy thunder, let them hasten away, in the name of Jesus.
194. Thou power that troubled the Egyptians, trouble my enemies, in the name of Jesus.
195. O gates of brass and bars of iron working against me, be broken, in the name of Jesus.
196. Let the rivers of my enemies be turned into wilderness, in the name of Jesus.
197. Set a wicked man over the wicked, in the name of Jesus.
198. Let the days of my enemies be cut off and let another take their office, in the name of Jesus.
199. As the enemy loves cursing, let it come unto him, in the name of Jesus.
200. As the enemy delights not in blessings, let it be far from him, in the name of Jesus.
201. As the enemy clothes himself with cursing like as with a garment, so let it come into his bowels like water and like oil into his bones, in the name of Jesus.
202. The wicked shall be grieved and his desires shall perish, in the name of Jesus.
203. I come against every form of barrenness in my life, in the name of Jesus.
204. Let all those who consult darkness against me, be disgraced, in the name of Jesus.

205. The Lord is on my side, I will not fear what can man do unto me, in the name of Jesus.

206. Depart from me, you evil doers, for I will keep the commandments of my God, in the name of Jesus.

207. Deliver me from the oppression of man, in the name of Jesus.

208. O righteous God, cut off the cords of the wicked, in the name of Jesus.

209. Let them be confounded and turned back that hate Zion, in the name of Jesus.

210. Let the wicked be as the grass upon the house tops which withers before it grows up, in the name of Jesus.

> Let their sword enter into their hearts and let their bows be broken, in the name of Jesus.

Prayer Watch

6

9:00 PM

PRAYER WATCH 6

9:00 PM

Confession -

Rev. 13:10: *He that leadeth into captivity shall go into captivity: he that killeth with the sword must be killed with the sword. Here is the patience and the faith of the saints.*

Praise Worship

Prayer Points:

1. Thank the Lord for He is the only One that answers prayers.
2. Every Haman assigned against my life, fall down and die, in the name of Jesus.
3. Every messenger of death assigned against my life, go back to your sender, in the name of Jesus.
4. Every agent of death buried inside my body, come out and die, in the name of Jesus.

5. Every gate of death assigned to swallow me, swallow your owner, in the name of Jesus.
6. Every plantation of death in my life, die, in the name of Jesus.
7. Every stronghold of death on my mind and imagination, be pulled down, in the name of Jesus.
8. By the resurrection of the Lord Jesus Christ, the power of death is broken upon my life, in the name of Jesus.
9. Every sting of death fashioned against my life, be neutralised by the blood of Jesus.
10. Every certificate of untimely death issued against my life, catch fire, in the name of Jesus.
11. I shall not die, but live to declare the works of God, in the name of Jesus.
12. The numbers of my days shall be fulfilled, in the name of Jesus.
13. Every damaged organ in my body, be repaired by fire, in the name of Jesus.
14. My bones shall not be broken through accident, in the name of Jesus.
15. Every power that does not want to see me around, fall down and die, in the name of Jesus.
16. My soul shall not see corruption of death through sickness, accident or calamity, in the name of Jesus.
17. I drink the blood of Jesus, let the life in the blood of Jesus flow into every organ of my body, in the name of Jesus.
18. My blood, by the blood of Jesus, be inoculated and immunised against the invasion of death, in thename of Jesus.
19. I eat of the flesh of Jesus, and I receive life into my body, in the name of Jesus.

Every power digging grave for me, enter therein, in the name of Jesus.

20. Every arrow of untimely death fashioned against my life, go back to your senders, in the name of Jesus.
21. Every power digging grave for me, enter therein, in the name of Jesus.
22. Vehicle of my transportation shall not become my coffin, in the name of Jesus.
23. I shall not journey into death, in the name of Jesus.
24. Every snare of death set up for my life, catch your owners, in the name of Jesus.
25. There shall be no sorrow of death in my family, in the name of Jesus.
26. Every shadow of death assigned against my life, scatter, in the name of Jesus.
27. Let the mark of the blood of Jesus wipe off every mark of death on my body, in the name of Jesus.
28. Every stronghold of untimely death fashioned against my life, be pulled down by fire, in the name of Jesus.
29. You wind of death, go back to your sender, in the name of Jesus.
30. Every spirit of depression and despair, die, in the name of Jesus.
31. Every wind of death, go back to your sender, in the name of Jesus.
32. Every satanic device to terminate my life, catch fire, in the name of Jesus.
33. Let the tokens of the liars to cut off my life be frustrated, in the name of Jesus.
34. Every pollution of death in the organ of my body, die, in the name of Jesus.
35. Let my blood be transfused with the blood of Jesus.
36. Every poison and contamination in my blood, be flushed out, in the name of Jesus.

37. Every tree of untimely death in my family line, my life is not your candidate, die, in the name of Jesus.
38. Every evil hunter of my soul, turn back and die, in the name of Jesus.
39. By the power in the blood of Jesus, I subdue death, oppression and violence, in the name of Jesus.
40. O God, I thank You for giving me life to replace death.
41. Let the teeth of the enemy over my life break, in the name of Jesus.
42. Every evil seed planted in my life by my place of birth, die, in the name of Jesus.
43. My glory, come out of the cage of evil location, in the name of Jesus.
44. O Lord, make all the rough places plain before me, in the name of Jesus.
45. Every ancient gate of my place of birth, locking up my progress, hear the word of the Lord, lift up your heads and open, in the name of Jesus.
46. Every evil power of my place of birth, die, in the name of Jesus.
47. My glory, what are you doing in the valley? Arise and shine, in the name of Jesus.
48. Every satanic father and every satanic mother, in the spirit realm, die, in the name of Jesus.
49. Let every covenant with the earth against my life be broken, in the name of Jesus.
50. Let every covenant with the sun, the moon and the stars against my life be broken, in the name of Jesus.
51. Let every covenant with the water against my life be broken, in the name of Jesus.
52. Everyone who has accepted witchcraft for my sake, be disgraced, in the name of Jesus.

53. Every power crippling against me, die, in the name of Jesus.
54. O Lord, release the rivers of life upon my dwelling, in the name of Jesus.
55. I shall not be a spiritual casualty, in the name of Jesus.
56. O Lord, take away my portions from casualty, in the name of Jesus.
57. My God, my life shall not be left with the wind, in the name of Jesus.
58. The meanderings of the enemy will not prosper in my life, in the name of Jesus.
59. Let the excesses of darkness be checked and stopped by fire, in the name of Jesus.
60. I break the law of death over my life, in the name of Jesus
61. Every covenant of death with this year concerning me, my family and my ministry, be broken, in the name of Jesus.
62. I am invisible to aggressive elements, in the name of Jesus.
63. My portion and water shall be secured, in the name of Jesus.
64. I destroy every magic in any house I have entered, in the name of Jesus.
65. Every evil power that has established authority in my family, be dismantled, in the name of the Jesus.
66. Wherever I go, satanic agents will not steal my portion, in the name of Jesus.
67. I command the sword of the Lord to rise against every enemy of my soul, in the name of Jesus.
68. Every biting demon, be silenced, in the name of Jesus.
69. Let the oil lost in my life be returned, in the name of Jesus.

70. I pull down every throne of iniquity, in the name of Jesus.
71. God will find rest in my life, in the name of Jesus.
72. Let the wall of challenges against my breakthroughs, break, in the name of Jesus.
73. My neck shall not be broken by territorial spirits, in the name of Jesus.
74. Blood poured on the ground will not eat me up, in the name of Jesus.
75. My portion is not with the dead, in the name of Jesus.
76. Every charm or concoction poured on the ground to subdue my life, I destroy you, in the name of Jesus.
77. I destroy the hand of every witch-doctor working against me, in the name of Jesus.
78. Any blood sacrifice against me, let the life in that blood be provoked to smite the enemies, in the name of Jesus.
79. O life that has been allowed to die through rituals against me, arise and strangulate your killers, in the name of Jesus.
80. I quench every anger energised through the land against me, in the name of Jesus.
81. I subjugate the power of witches, in the name of Jesus.
82. Every alignment of witches against my life, be destroyed, in the name of Jesus.
83. Every conglomeration of witches, be melted, in the name of Jesus.
84. I loose my life from every witchcraft poisoning, in the name of Jesus.
85. I break the poison in my life, in the name of Jesus.

Prayer
WATCH

7

12:00AM

PRAYER WATCH 7
12:00 AM

Confession -
2 Samuel 2:6-10; Isaiah 7:7-11

Praise Worship

Prayer Points:
1. I render every aggressive altar impotent, in the name of Jesus.
2. Every evil altar erected against me, be disgraced, in the name of Jesus.
3. Anything done against my life under demonic anointing, be nullified, in the name of Jesus.
4. I curse every local altar fashioned against me, in the name of Jesus.
5. Let the hammer of the Almighty God smash every evil altar erected against me, in the name of Jesus.

6. O Lord, send Your fire to destroy every evil altar fashioned against me, in the name of Jesus.
7. Every evil priest ministering against me at the evil altar, receive the sword of God, in the name of Jesus.
8. Let the thunder of God smite every evil priest working against me on the evil altar and burn them to ashes, in the name of Jesus.
9. Let every satanic priest ministering against me at evil altars fall down and die, in the name of Jesus.
10. Any hand that wants to retaliate or arrest me because of all these prayers I am praying, dry up and wither, in the name of Jesus.
11. Every stubborn evil altar priest, drink your own blood, in the name of Jesus.
12. I repossess my possession stolen by the evil altar, in the name of Jesus.
13. I withdraw my name from every evil altar, in the name of Jesus.
14. I withdraw my blessings from every evil altar, in the name of Jesus.
15. I withdraw my breakthroughs from every evil altar, in the name of Jesus.
16. I withdraw my glory from every evil altar, in the name of Jesus.
17. I withdraw my prosperity from every evil altar, in the name of Jesus.
18. I withdraw anything representing me from every evil altar, in the name of Jesus.
19. Mention the organ that you know is not behaving the way it should. When you have done this, begin

to say, "I withdraw you from every evil altar, in the name of Jesus." Say this seven hot times.
20. Let the wind of the Holy Spirit bring every scattered bone together now, in the name of Jesus.
21. I use the blood of Jesus to reverse every poor record of the past about my life, in the name of Jesus.
22. I refuse to accept satanic substitute for my destiny, in the name of Jesus.
23. I refuse to be caged by the enemy of good things, in the name of Jesus.
24. Let every internal coffin in my life receive the fire of God and be burnt dpown roasted now, in the name of Jesus.
25. Every destiny-paralysing power fashioned against my destiny, fall down and die, in the name of Jesus.
26. Every inherited evil limitation in any area of my life, depart now, in the name of Jesus.
27. Every architect of spiritual coffins, I command you to fall down and die, in the name of Jesus.
28. Every cloud of uncertainty, clear away now, in the name of Jesus.
29. I refuse to be converted to a living dead, in the name of Jesus.
30. Let every effect of evil laying on of hands and shaking of evil hands on y life, be nullified, in the name of Jesus.
31. Every satanic consultation concerning my life, be nullified, in the name of Jesus.
32. Every decision taken against my life by witchcraft spirits, be nullified, in the name of Jesus.
33. I reject aborted victories in every area of my life, in the name of Jesus.

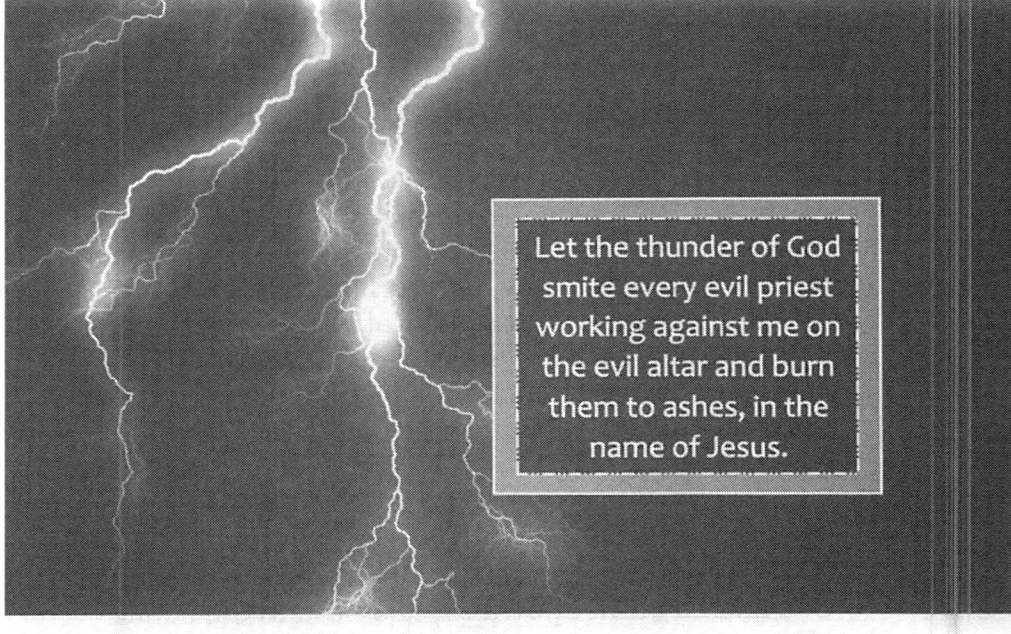

> Let the thunder of God smite every evil priest working against me on the evil altar and burn them to ashes, in the name of Jesus.

34. Every caged star, be released now, in the name of Jesus.
35. My imagination and dreams will not be used against me, in the name of Jesus.
36. O God, arise and visit all the shrines assigned against me with thunder and earthquake, in the name of Jesus.
37. All satanic altars, erected against my destiny, be overthrown by fire, in the name of Jesus.
38. O God, arise and set unquenchable fire upon every coven of darkness assigned against me, in Jesus' name.
39. All images, carved against my life, break into pieces after the order of Dragon, in the name of Jesus.
40. O God, arise and cause confusion in the camp of my enemies, in the name of Jesus.
41. I decree that my oppressors shall consult their powers in their confusion, but there will be no response, in the name of Jesus.

42. Holy Ghost fire, arise and stir up civil war in the camp of my enemies, in the name of Jesus.
43. I command every satanic intermediary working against me to loose heart, in the name of Jesus.
44. O God, arise and bring the plans of my oppressors to nothing, in the name of Jesus.
45. My Father, set up a fierce king against my oppressors and let the king treat them with great torture, in the name of Jesus.
46. Let the power of God intimidate and frustrate all diviners assigned against me, in the name of Jesus.
47. O God, arise and wipe out the understanding and memory of my stubborn pursuers, in the name of Jesus.
48. O God, pour out the spirit of dizziness upon all evil spiritual consultants speaking against me, in Jesus' name.
49. Let these evil spiritual consultants stagger in all they do as a drunkard staggers in his vomit, in Jesus' name.
50. By the power in the blood of Jesus, let all soothsayers, witch doctors and enchanters arranged against me be cut off, in the name of Jesus.
51. O heavens, o earth, hear the word of the Lord. You must not execute the counsel of my enemies, in the name of Jesus.
52. O God, pass through the camp of my enemies with affliction and drain the anointing of wickedness, in the name of Jesus.

53. Every power assigned to wreck my destiny, your end has come, die, in the name of Jesus.
54. I de-programme and cancel all negative prophecies pronounced against me, in the name of Jesus.
55. O Lord, guide me into the mysteries of my life.
56. O Lord, give me the keys to unlock the hidden riches of secret places.
57. All ancient doors that have hindered the plan of God for my life, be unlocked by fire, in the name of Jesus.
58. I destroy every agreement made at covens and satanic centres against me, in the name of Jesus.
59. Every secret code, evil registers and archives of the enemy in my place of birth, be burnt to ashes, in the name of Jesus.
60. O God, arise and cast abominable filth upon witches and wizards and turn them to a laughing stock, in the name of Jesus.
61. Let the tables of witches and wizards become snares unto them, in the name of Jesus.
62. Let the eyes of witches monitoring my life be blinded, in the name of Jesus.
63. Let the covens of witchcraft become desolate, let there be no one to dwell in them, in the name of Jesus.
64. I command the crash-landing of witches and wizards assigned against my breakthrough, in the name of Jesus.
65. I command the sun to smite my oppressors in the day and the moon and stars to smite them at night, in the name of Jesus.

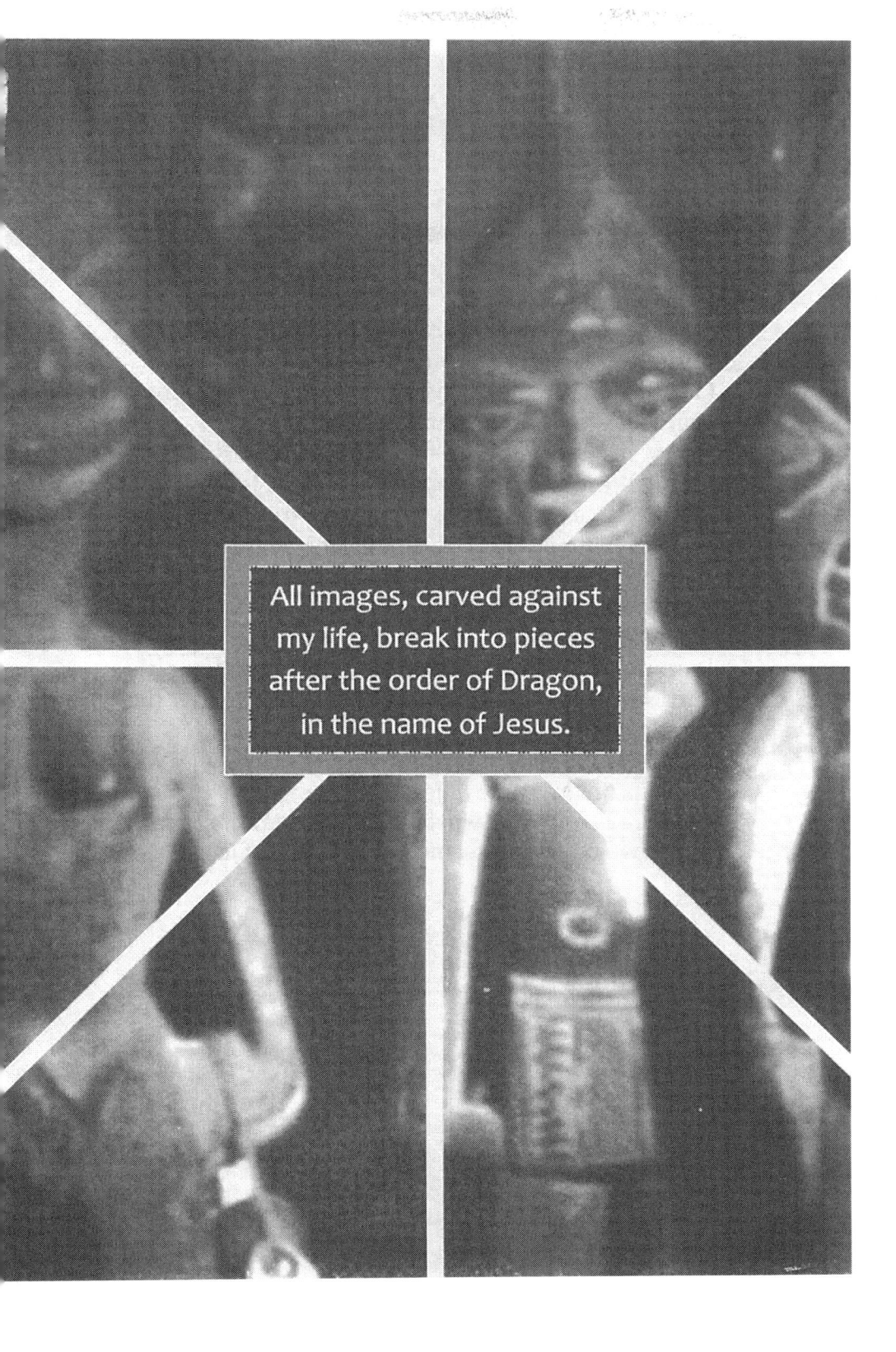

All images, carved against my life, break into pieces after the order of Dragon, in the name of Jesus.

66. I command the stars in their courses to fight against my stubborn pursuers, in the name of Jesus.
67. O God, arise, roar and prevail over my enemies, in the name of Jesus.
68. Let the gathering of the wicked against me be harvested for destruction, in the name of Jesus.
69. O God, arise and hang every Haman assigned against my life, in the name of Jesus.
70. Every stumbling block to God's prophetic agenda for my life, be rooted out, in the name of Jesus.
71. All negative words that have been spoken against me by evil men, die, in the name of Jesus.
72. All evil records, evil marriage certificates and registers that are kept in satanic archives against me, be wiped off by the blood of Jesus.
73. I programme divine health, divine favour, long life and spiritual advancement into my life by the power in the blood of Jesus.
74. I ship-wreck every spiritual ship carting away my benefits, in the name of Jesus.
75. O God, arise and lay waste all the operations of dark forces working against me, in the name of Jesus.

Other Publications by Dr. D. K. Olukoya

1. 20 Marching Orders To Fulfill Your Destiny
2. 30 Prophetic Arrows From Heaven
3. 30 Things The Anointing Can Do For You
4. Abraham's Children in Bondage
5. A-Z of Complete Deliverance
6. Basic Prayer Patterns
7. Be Prepared
8. Bewitchment must Die
9. Biblical Principles of Dream Interpretation
10. Born Great, But Tied Down
11. Breaking Bad Habits
12. Breakthrough Prayers For Business Professionals
13. Bringing Down The Power of God
14. Brokenness
15. Can God Trust You?
16. Command The Morning
17. Connecting to The God of Breakthroughs
18. Consecration Commitment & Loyalty
19. Contending For The Kingdom
20. Criminals In The House Of God
21. Dancers At The Gate of Death
22. Dealing Destiny Vultures
23. Dealing With Destiny Thieves
24. Dealing With Hidden Curses
25. Dealing With Local Satanic Technology
26. Dealing With Satanic Exchange
27. Dealing With The Evil Powers Of Your Father's House
28. Dealing With Tropical Demons
29. Dealing With Unprofitable Roots
30. Dealing With Witchcraft Barbers
31. Deep Secrets, Deep Deliverance

Other Publications by Dr. D. K. Olukoya

32. Deliverance By Fire
33. Deliverance From Evil Foundation
34. Deliverance From Spirit Husband And Spirit Wife
35. Deliverance From The Limiting Powers
36. Deliverance of The Brain
37. Deliverance Of The Conscience
38. Deliverance Of The Head
39. Deliverance of The Tongue
40. Deliverance: God's Medicine Bottle
41. Destiny Clinic
42. Destroying Satanic Masks
43. Disgracing Soul Hunters
44. Divine Military Training
45. Divine Prescription For Your Total Immunity
46. Divine Yellow Card
47. Dominion Prosperity
48. Drawers Of Power From The Heavenlies
49. Evil Appetite
50. Evil Umbrella
51. Facing Both Ways
52. Failure In The School Of Prayer
53. Fire For Life's Journey
54. For We Wrestle ...
55. Freedom Indeed
56. God's Key To A Happy Life
57. Healing Through Prayers
58. Holiness Unto The Lord
59. Holy Cry
60. Holy Fever
61. Hour Of Decision

62. How To Obtain Personal Deliverance
63. How To Pray When Surrounded By The Enemies
64. I Am Moving Forward
65. Idols Of The Heart
66. Igniting Your Inner Fire
67. Is This What They Died For?
68. Kill Your Goliath By Fire
69. Killing The Serpent of Frustration
70. Let Fire Fall
71. Let God Answer By Fire
72. Limiting God
73. Lord, Behold Their Threatening
74. Madness of The Heart
75. Making Your Way Through The Traffic Jam of Life
76. Meat For Champions
77. Medicine For Winners
78. My Burden For The Church
79. Open Heavens Through Holy Disturbance
80. Overpowering Witchcraft
81. Paralysing The Riders And The Horse
82. Personal Spiritual Check-Up
83. Possessing The Tongue of Fire
84. Power Against Coffin Spirits
85. Power Against Destiny Quenchers
86. Power Against Dream Criminals
87. Power Against Local Wickedness
88. Power Against Marine Spirits
89. Power Against Spiritual Terrorists
90. Power Against The Mystery of Wickedness
91. Power Against Unclean Spirits
92. Power Must Change Hands
93. Power of Brokenness

94. Power To Disgrace The Oppressors
95. Power To Recover Your Birthright
96. Power To Recover Your Lost Glory
97. Power To Shut Satanic Doors
98. Pray Your Way To Breakthroughs
99. Prayer Strategies For Singles
100. Prayer Is The Battle
101. Prayer Rain
102. Prayer To Kill Enchantment
103. Prayer To Make You Fulfill Your Divine Destiny
104. Prayer Warfare Against 70 Mad Spirits
105. Prayers For Open Heavens
106. Prayers To Destroy Diseases And Infirmities
107. Prayers To Move From Minimum To Maximum
108. Praying Against Foundational Poverty
109. Praying Against The Spirit Of The Valley
110. Praying In The Storm
111. Praying To Destroy Satanic Roadblocks
112. Praying To Dismantle Witchcraft
113. Principles of Conclusive Prayers
114. Principles Of Prayer
115. Raiding The House of The Strongman
116. Release From Destructive Covenants
117. Revoking Evil Decrees
118. Safeguarding Your Home
119. Satanic Diversion Of The Black Race
120. Secrets of Spiritual Growth And Maturity
121. Setting The Covens Ablaze
122. Seventy Rules of Spiritual Warfare
123. Seventy Sermons To Preach To Your Destiny
124. Silencing The Birds Of Darkness

125. Slave Masters
126. Slaves Who Love Their Chains
127. Smite The Enemy And He Will Flee
128. Speaking Destruction Unto The Dark Rivers
129. Spiritual Education
130. Spiritual Growth And Maturity
131. Spiritual Warfare And The Home
132. Stop Them Before They Stop You
133. Strategic Praying
134. Strategy Of Warfare Praying
135. Students In The School Of Fear
136. Symptoms Of Witchcraft Attack
137. Taking The Battle To The Enemy's Gate
138. The Amazing Power of Faith
139. The Baptism of Fire
140. The Battle Against The Spirit Of Impossibility
141. The Chain Breaker
142. The Dinning Table Of Darkness
143. The Enemy Has Done This
144. The Evil Cry Of Your Family Idol
145. The Fire Of Revival
146. The Gateway To Spiritual Power
147. The Great Deliverance
148. The Hidden Viper
149. The Internal Stumbling Block
150. The Lord is A Man of War
151. The Mystery Of Mobile Curses
152. The Mystery Of The Mobile Temple
153. The Power of Aggressive Prayer Warriors
154. The Power of Priority
155. The Prayer Eagle

156. The Pursuit Of Success
157. The Scale of The Almighty
158. The School of Tribulation
159. The Seasons Of Life
160. The Secrets Of Greatness
161. The Serpentine Enemies
162. The Skeleton In Your Grandfather's Cupboard
163. The Slow Learners
164. The Snake In The Power House
165. The Spirit Of The Crab
166. The Star Hunters
167. The Star In Your Sky
168. The Terrible Agenda
169. The Tongue Trap
170. The Unconquerable Power
171. The University of Champions
172. The Unlimited God
173. The Vagabond Spirit
174. The Way Of Divine Encounter
175. The Wealth Transfer Agenda
176. Tied Down In The Spirits
177. Too Hot To Handle
178. Turnaround Breakthrough
179. Unprofitable Foundations
180. Victory Over Satanic Dreams
181. Victory Over Your Greatest Enemies
182. Violent Prayers Against Stubborn Situations
183. War At The Edge Of Breakthroughs
184. Wasted At The Market Square of Life
185. Wasting The Wasters
186. Wealth Must Change Hands

187. What You Must Know About The House Fellowship
188. When God Is Silent
189. When The Battle is from Home
190. When The Deliverer Need Deliverance
191. When The Enemy Hides
192. When Things Get Hard
193. When You Are Knocked Down
194. When You Are Under Attack
195. When You Need A Change
196. Where Is Your Faith?
197. While Men Slept
198. Woman! Thou Art Loosed.
199. Your Battle And Your Strategy
200. Your Foundation And Destiny
201. Your Mouth And Your Deliverance
202. Your Mouth And Your Warfare

YORUBA PUBLICATIONS

1. Adura Agbayori
2. Adura Ti Nsi Oke Ni' di
3. Ojo Adura

FRENCH PUBLICATIONS

1. Bilan Spirituel Personnel
2. Cantique Des Contiques
3. Commander Le Matin
4. Comment Recevior La Delivrance Du Mari Et Femme De Nuit
5. Cpmment Se Delivrer Soi-meme

Other Publications by Dr. D. K. Olukoya

6. Demanteler La Sorcellerie
7. En Finir Avec Les Forces Malefiques De La Maison De Ton Pere
8. Espirit De Vagabondage
9. Femme Tu Es Liberee
10. Frappez l'adversaire Et Il Fuira
11. L'etoile Dans Votre Ciel
12. La Deliverance De La Tete
13. La Deliverance: Le Flacon De Medicament Dieu
14. La Deviation Satanique De La Race Noire
15. Le Combat Spirituel Et Le Foyer
16. Le Mauvais Cri Des Idoles
17. Le Programme De Tranfert De Richesse
18. Les Etudiants A l'ecole De La Peur
19. Les Saisons De La Vie
20. Les Strategies De Prieres Pour Les Celibataires
21. Ne Grand Mais Lie
22. Pluie De Priere
23. Pouvoir Contre Les Demond Tropicaux
24. Povoir Contre Les Terrorites Spirituel
25. Prier Jusqu'a Remporter La Victoire
26. Priere De Percees Pour Les Hommes D'affaires
27. Priere Pour Detruire Les Maladies Et Infirmites
28. Prieres Violentes Pour Humilier Les Problemes Opiniatres
29. Prieres De Comat Contre 70 Espirits Dechanines
30. Quand Les Choses Deviennent Difficiles
31. Que l'envoutement Perisse
32. Revoquer Les Decrets Malefiques
33. Se Liberer Des Alliances Malefiques
34. Ton Combat Et Ta Strategie
35. Victoires Sur Les Reves Sataniques
36. Votre Fondement Et Votre Destin

ANNUAL 70 DAYS PRAYER AND FASTING PUBLICATIONS

1. Prayers That Bring Miracles
2. Let God Answer By Fire
3. Prayers To Mount With Wings As Eagles
4. Prayers That Bring Explosive Increase
5. Prayers For Open Heavens
6. Prayers To Make You Fulfill Your Divine Destiny
7. Prayers That Make God To Answer And Fight By Fire
8. Prayers That Bring Unchallengeable Victory And Breakthrough Rainfall Bombardments
9. Prayers That Bring Dominion Prosperity And Uncommon Success
10. Prayers That Bring Power And Overflowing Progress
11. Prayers That Bring Laughter And Enlargement Breakthroughs
12. Prayers That Bring Uncommon Favour And Breakthroughs
13. Prayers That Bring Unprecedented Greatness And Unmatchable Increase
14. Prayers That Bring Awesome Testimonies And Turn Around Breakthroughs
15. Prayers That Bring Glorious Restoration
16. Prayers That Bring Unrivaled Lifting

Publications By Pastor (Mrs.) Shade Olukoya

1. Daughters of Philip
2. I Decree An Uncommon Change
3. Power To Fulfil Your Destiny
4. Principles of A Successful Marriage
5. The Call of God
6. When Your Destiny Is Under Attack
7. Woman of Wonder
8. Violence Against Negative Voices

The Books, Tapes and CDs (Audio and Video) All Obtainable At:

- **MFM International Bookshop**
  13, Olasimbo Street, Onike, Yaba, Lagos

- **MFM Prayer City**
  Km 12, Lagos/Ibadan Expressway

- **Battle Cry Christian Ministries**
  322, Herbert Macaulay Way, Sabo, Yaba, Lagos
  Phone: 01 8044415, 0803 304 4239

- 54, Akeju Street, off Shipeolu Street
  Palmgrove, Lagos

- **All MFM Churches Nationwide**

- **All Leading Christian Bookstores**

- **Battle Cry Christian Ministries**
  Abuja Zonal Office & Bookshop
  No 4, Nasarawa Street, Block A,
  Shop 4, Garki Old Market.
  Phone: 08135865868, 08159103039.

Printed in Great Britain
by Amazon